GopherHaul

Extreme Lawn Care Business Tips.

Unfiltered, unedited, and a little rough.
A collection of landscaping & lawn care business
lessons I've learned along the way.

I see so many new lawn care businesses get started only to fail a short time later because the entrepreneurs didn't educate themselves enough about their field. Here is a collection of lessons I learned that will give your business a better chance at success.

By Steve Low

Host of The GopherHaul Lawn Care Business Show

and the Gopher Lawn Care Business Forum.

Table Of Contents

Special thanks to Gopher Lawn Care Software.

This book would not have been possible without the help and guidance from all our friends and business owners we have met over the years on our Gopher Lawn Care Business Forum as well as others.

Also thank you to the staff at Gopher Lawn Care Business Software for making all of this possible.

Lawn Care Software

PROBLEM: Scheduling & billing repetitive jobs is tedious and time consuming.

SOLUTION: Gopher Billing & Scheduling Software allows you to Quickly and Easily schedule jobs and create invoices.

Gopher Landscape Billing and Scheduling Software simplifies the task of scheduling your lawn care jobs and billing your customers. Simply set up your jobs at the beginning of the season and let Gopher handle the rest. With Gopher, you can print out a list of scheduled jobs for each day and then automatically print invoices after those jobs have been completed.

Download your free trial of Gopher Billing & Scheduling Software at http://www.gophersoftware.com

Continue your reading.

I have more great information on running a lawn care business in my other books, **"Stop Lowballing! A Lawn Care Business Owner's Guide To Success."**

Some of the topics discussed in the book: - How to start up your lawn care business. - Finding your niche and finding profits. - Lawn Care Equipment. - Pricing & Estimating Lawn Care Jobs. - Dealing With Customers. - Dealing With Employees. - Lawn Care Marketing Secrets. - Lawn Care Business Tips. - Getting Commercial Accounts without commercial references. - Pitfalls of Commercial Accounts. And more.

The GopherHaul Lawn Care Marketing & Landscaping Business Show Episode Guide.

Topics discuss include: How to raise start up capital. Seasonal marketing ideas. What to do when your largest client leaves? What's better to use, postcards or brochures? How to build your customer base with referrals? Gain one customer then lose one customer. How to stop it? How to pre-qualify customers when they call? How to bid jobs. What should you include in a commercial lawn care bid? What newspaper ads work best? How to buy a lawn care business. Tips on buying used lawn care equipment. And much more.

How to get customers for your landscaping and lawn care business all year long. Volume 1.

Anyone can start a lawn care business, the tricky part is finding customers. Learn how in this book.

New lawn care business owners were polled and 33% of them said the toughest part about running their business was finding customers. This book shows you how to get new lawn care customers. Don't start from scratch and try to re-create the wheel. Learn what works and what doesn't.

Volume #1 discusses: Getting started, choosing a business name, harnessing employees to sell, community marketing ideas, free rentals to offer, hosting events to get exposure, volunteer projects to build goodwill, how to get residential and commercial customers (including sample letters). Bikini lawn care, getting in your local paper, marketing on price, publicity stunts & media attention, organic lawn care marketing, reaching out to realtors, turning hobbies into marketing ideas, seasonal marketing ideas that work.

How to get customers for your landscaping and lawn care business all year long. Volume 2.

Anyone can start a lawn care business but most get stuck finding customers and they give up their new venture too quickly. Why struggle trying to learn how to gain new lawn care customers the hard way? This book gives you lawn care marketing ideas that are being used by your competitors. It also talks about what marketing ideas don't work.

Volume #2 discusses: The most effective lawn care business marketing methods. How to track your ads, the best ways to utilize: billboards, brochures, business cards, buying lawn care customers, clubs & organizations, coupons & gift cards, co-marketing, door hangers, going door to door, flyers, internet marketing, lawn signs, customer letters, direct mailing, newsletters, newspaper ad, phone book advertising, phones & telemarketing, postcards, referrals, sports, testimonials, trade shows, truck & trailer advertising, word of mouth.

The Big Lawn Care Marketing Book

This book contains 470 pages of marketing ideas to help your lawn care & landscaping business grow.

The Big Lawn Care Marketing Book contains volume 1 & 2 of my other books "How to get customers for your landscaping and lawn care business all year long."

The landscaping and lawn care business plan startup guide.

If you ever had thought about starting your own lawn care or landscaping business but weren't sure how to go about putting together a business plan, this book will show you examples of lawn care business plans created on the Gopher Lawn Care Business Forum. The author of this lawn care business book is the host of The GopherHaul Lawn Care Business Show and the Gopher Lawn Care Business Forum.

Inside is a step by step guide on how to make a landscape or lawn care business plan with real life examples including income and expense projections as well as customer acquisition goals. This lawn care business book is a great tool to help you improve your odds of finding success.

How to use Gopher Lawn Care Business Billing & Scheduling Software.

Learn how to manage your lawn care and landscaping business easier with this powerful software.

A Rebellious Teenagers Guide To Starting A Landscaping & Lawn Care Business.

When you are a teenager you have a lot of rebellious energy. Why not take that energy, harness it to be productive, and make money! This book will show you how to succeed in starting your own landscaping & lawn care business. I cover the basics of how to register your business to advanced topics like incentives to get employees to sell more.

You can order these books through the following websites:

http://www.gophersoftware.com

http://www.gopherforum.com

http://www.amazon.com

Getting started.

Biggest lawn care business start up mistakes.

When you get your lawn care business started there are plenty of things that can go wrong. Are you buying the wrong mower? What about your landscape trailer. How about your lawn care marketing plan? Consider the following problems other lawn care business owners went through and learn from their mistakes. I asked this question on the Gopher Lawn Care Business Forum, what were the biggest mistakes you made starting out and what do you wish you could have done differently?

Here are some of the responses.

- "The first mistake I made was buying a crappy trailer. Second was not getting a zero turn mower.

The fact is that I use a tractor at the moment to mow lawns. If I would have borrowed the money for a zero turn, I would probably be debt free now and making money with my lawn care business because I'd be able to mow a lot faster."

- "Here is one I can come up with. I purchased a Dodge Ram 1500 6 ft. bed for my lawn care business. It was doing fine until my lawn care customers started asking for other services. Landscaping, Hardscape and etc...

Next purchase will be a small dump truck."

- "A commercial ZT lawn mower easily doubles (if not more) the productivity of a residential grade tractor mower. It does a better job, faster with a lot less driver fatigue. I've found with every upgrade that made me faster, I ended up with blank space in my schedule at first.

You will then find you have more time on your hands so you get creative on your advertising & marketing instead of just working. Every time, I've found ways to fill the schedule in again. More work = more money. Then I upgrade again, more equipment, more employees etc. This spring should be more everything. Time for a 2nd lawn mowing crew! I could just as easily still be a one man lawn care operation today running the residential tractor I had for my lawn prior to opening up the business. I'd be working my butt off on like 20 lawn care accounts for a little money. Instead I went big & grew big (Still growing at around 120 lawn care accounts currently.) The old adage "it takes money to make money" does apply here in this industry too.

Sorry to go off on a tangent but I think it accurately explains the consequences of working with inferior gear."

- "That is exactly why I am looking to get a ZTR as fast as I can, but before that, I need to afford a truck that can pull my trailer so I can pull that ZTR. It takes money to spend money but my lawn care equipment is gonna have to be upgraded sometime in the near future."

- "I understand the dilemma, Some may not have the financial means to do so right away & hey everyone's gotta start somewhere right? But to build your lawn care business quickly it takes a little financial risk & investment. Ya know if I have to bet my hard earned money on something, betting on myself & my performance is a good bet for me any day! So yeah I extended some money on the bet I could make the business fly, if it failed it would have been my fault & my fault alone so it was a safe bet for me. My family's welfare was on the line, I don't fail under pressure."

- "I think one of the biggest mistakes for any new landscaping business is not advertising enough. The biggest advertising you can do is put your name on your trailer and truck. Every time you go out and do something whether it be a job or just take a drive you will be an advertising machine. Every new lawn care business has to take advantage of this.

You have to be in all your local phone books. The ad size is up to you and how much your willing to spend but at least get your number in there. As far as tracking where your customers come from. I normally ask the customer how did you hear about us or you can put codes on your advertising or get a couple phone lines. Have 1 line for the phone book 1 line for your vehicle ads and 1 line for any flyers you put out."

- "One mistake I found was spreading myself too thin both geographically and in the services offered.

My first year in the lawn care business I accepted clients all over town. I even had customers 25+ miles away. Travel time can kill a lawn care business. In addition to wasting time and gas, the downtime of being in your truck knocks you off your stride.

Also, I think lawn care business owners should focus on a small number of services offered. I am sure most people here have been asked to put up mailboxes and tighten outdoor light fixtures.

There is nothing wrong with making extra money during winter with these add-ons but taking time away from your standard services can be time consuming. Have you ever agreed to install a mailbox not realizing you don't have the right tools? You look around your truck and see two flat head screwdrivers and not a philips. A "quick" $25 job can turn into 90 minutes of frustration. During that time you could have done two residential lawns. If you're going to offer these services, make sure you have all the tools and the know-how to complete the job efficiently."

–   "Here are some of the problems I ran into.
1. Buying a 2WD truck (should have spent the extra money and got 4×4)
2. Buying a wider trailer. The max deck size I can put on my trailer is 52"
3. Not giving myself enough time for the office. I exhausted myself in the field and couldn't concentrate in the office. This year I will be delegating more office work to my office manager aka my wife."

Keep these mistakes others have had in mind as you develop your lawn care business and you will find yourself well advanced.

A bad way to start your lawn care business.

I am lucky to talk with many new lawn care business owners who are just getting started. Most of the time they seem to ask two questions. How do I get commercial accounts and how do I figure out how much to charge to mow a lawn. Let's look at this example.

One lawn care business owner wrote "My husband and I are just starting our business. He is plowing now as a sub-contractor. I know we need to get going getting landscaping business for the Spring, but we have no idea where to start. How do we go about getting commercial business? How do we know when they are accepting bids? Do we just call and ask? Or is there a certain time of year that everyone does it? I will be doing most of the lawn care, and he will be doing pruning, hardscapes, anything more difficult. He went to school for landscaping and has been doing it for almost 10 years. I went to school for business, so I'll be taking care of that end of it, but I love to be outside too!

I am new at this and I am trying to find out what the the going rates are for mowing, edging, blowing, and mulching.

Any advice is appreciated!"

Let's start with the topic of going for commercial customers when you are just getting started. It seems most lawn care business owners would advise against it and here are some insights as to why.

One business owner wrote "you can make more per man hour on residential lawn care customers versus commercial work, so you might want to stick with residential lawn care customers for a while."

Another said "Getting your feet wet with residential lawn care clients is preferable for many lawn care businesses.

If you slightly mis-bid a residential lawn care customer or two you can easily recover. However a bad bid on a large scale commercial lawn care account can sink you before you even get out of the gate.

Start small and build gradually. Slow and steady wins the race.

As far as timing for getting clients; right now is the best time. Customers are already beginning to think about late Winter clean up of their yards."

Next when it comes to pricing, you should base your price on your costs. Now I know most new lawn care business owners are not interested in hearing that. They want to hear a solid figure. They want to hear charge $30 a lawn or $35 to mow. You can call up local lawn care business owners in your area and get a few bids to cut your home lawn or a friends lawn to get an idea but that can be a bad idea on many levels. Let's see why.

"I personally feel calling other lawn care business owners is a lousy method of determining what the going lawn care rate is.

First of all, you are wasting time and expense of others in the lawn care business. If you have no intention of giving them business don't make them come to your property to give an estimate…that's just wrong.

Secondly; how do you know what their costs are? If they are lowballers doing $20 lawns, will you drop your price to $18 just to undercut them? This method gives a completely skewed idea of the profit potential of lawn care if you provide professional service and they are hacks.

Lastly; this is not a good way to make local friends in the business. How would you feel if you spent 30 minutes of your time driving to an estimate and speaking with the "customer" only to see him the next day with a lawn mower in his truck? It wouldn't make you feel good."

Keep all these things in mind when you are just starting your lawn care business.

Suggestions for a new lawn care business trying to break into the marketplace.

There is a huge void in business knowledge that exists in our society. Most of us never get any training on how to run a lawn care business, or how to build a lawn care business. If you are a new business owner you are hit with a double whammy. You don't know much about the service you are providing and then you don't know much about business. So I asked this question on the Gopher Lawn Care Business Forum, what suggestions do you have for new lawn care business owners who are trying to break into the marketplace?

One of our forum members said "this is a wonderful industry we all work in, and a very competitive one, and someone new to it needs to take the right steps. The majority of lawn care business owners have come into the industry as a 'career change.' Some with no experience, but perhaps cutting their own lawn or the neighbors. The first thing I would recommend is to get educated in the industry. Anyone can push a lawn mower, or weed a garden. But do you know:

- How much to cut?
- When to cut and when not to?
- The types of grass you deal with?

- Watering and bylaw restrictions?
- What types of weeds you are pulling?
- What types of fertilizers to use and when?
- Plant ID?
- Insects and disease?

Those are just some of the areas that you need to know. Now I know that most people have learned all of that through experience. But wouldn't you rather have the upper hand? Especially that you are new to the industry? A company that can offer the answers as well as the service is key. I have seen companies out there buy all new equipment, spend thousands on marketing and get a client list well over 1000…just to go out of business the following year. Simply because they could not provide what their clients needed to know."

These are very good points. It is worth noting and researching each of these topics as you go to improve your knowledge base.

A bad economy is a great time to start a lawn care business.

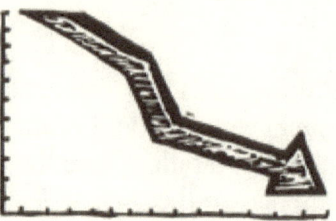

Are we in a rough patch now with our economy? I would say so and it's most likely going to get worse before it gets better. But you don't have to be a puppet in someone else's show. Now is a great time to start your own lawn care business. It's something you can do on the side, in the evenings or on weekends to get started. Why not prepare yourself now to take control of your own destiny if the job you work at starts to sputter? This is exactly what we were talking about in a post at the Gopher Lawn Care Business Forum.

A forum member wrote and said "Hello to all. I am a new member and I live in the great state of Florida. I have watching the Gopherhaul Lawn Care Business Shows online and have learned quite a bit. I do not have my own business but have spent the last three days reading and learning from all the members I just had to join and get in on some of the discussions.

I do have a couple of questions. We are in the beginning of November. Is it to late to start up a lawn care business? What advice would any one give to someone who wants to start up but has very little money. I am a homeowner. I own a 2 in one weed eater/edger, push lawn mower, blower (electric). Is it to late in the season or should I just wait till spring to start up? Also how much should I charge for mowing and edging yards. The economy is bad for everyone so I do not want to overprice and get no business but do not want to under price and make no money. I just need some good advice on how to go about getting things rolling."

I would say it is never too late to start because ultimately the later you start the earlier you are getting a jump on next year. There are many services you can offer in the slow months.

I would also start only with what you have and experiment. See if anyone on your block or in your local neighborhood is looking for lawn care. Get some business cards made and start handing them out.

If you are stuck coming up with basic prices on what the going rate in your area is for lawn mowing and edging, since you are a home owner why not call up a handful of local lawn care businesses, ask them for an estimate and have them cut your lawn. This way you can figure a range and then get started either in the low, middle or higher end of that spectrum. If you find yourself landing a lot of estimates, you might want to raise your prices. If you find you are not winning many lawn care bids, you should then lower your prices.

Are you a member of any local social organizations that you can harness to help get the word out too for you? What got you interested in starting your own lawn care business?

"I have thought about doing lawn care but never serious like I am now. The economy is what got me into starting this business. I have a full time night shift truck driving job and like so many companies things are just getting slower and slower so I am seeking independence for myself and my family because left and right big name companies and banks are closing or downsizing. So I am not gonna sit around and let my employer try to dictate me and my family life."

Excellent! Are you handy? Can you do light construction projects around the house? Would you consider offering handyman services to your local area? Also have you thought about how you are going to promote your business?

"I can do a little bit here and there, I am a very fast learner and to market the idea I was considering using the free flyers that I see posted on your site."

Good! Being able to do a lot of odd jobs for homeowners can really help you make it through the slower winter months and then you can potentially bring these customers along for lawn care in the next year.

Go through the free flyer section and see which really get you thinking. There are many many marketing ideas in there.

Also why not decorate your home for the holidays and put a small sign out front that you offer outdoor holiday decoration services as well? Then hand out flyers in your area that you offer this service. Make sure all your friends and family know you are going into business. Give them all business cards and ask them to hand out some business cards for you.

Remember, it's never too late or too early to start your lawn care business. The right time is always now.

Lawn care business advice from a teenage entrepreneur.

I know there are a lot of teenagers who are avid readers of the Gopher Lawn Care Business Forum and I am sure they are constantly looking for inspiration. One of our forum members who is is a teen himself has given us some great insight after ending his first full season running his lawn care business. When he started his business, he wasn't old enough to drive so a family member helped him by driving his truck from job to job. I do hope this story inspires others to think big.

"I want to update you guys on what I've been up to this year. Things have gone great! Gross profit is over three times what it was last year. I ended mowing this year with about 40 weekly mowing customers. I have an employee, who is a retired gentleman and a very hard worker."

Great job this year! What lessons have you learned so far this year that you can share with others just getting started out?

"There are a ton of things I have learned. This year was an eye-opener for me. I was busy all year, never struggling to get lawn care work. I really worked myself hard this year, but it is all paying off.

1. **Develop Relationships**. I got to meet the owner of the biggest nursery/supply yard around here. He started out just like I am. I do all my plant purchases there, etc. I walked in one Saturday afternoon, very close to their closing time, and I really needed a delivery. They took care of it. I will never forget that, because they came through for me, so I could get this job done. That means a lot to me, and its how I like to treat people.

2. As the old say goes says, **Shit happens**. Don't get frustrated. I had a day where I blew a trailer tire on the side of a major highway, had no spare, then I missed my exit getting back into town, had to drive an extra twenty minutes, then had to go back to school, get my school schedule, drive back to the town I got off the highway at, had to go back to town, then back to landscape supply shop, where I started my day off at. I traveled 150 miles that day. I had an employee on the clock, etc. It sucked, but it could have been worst.

3. **Learn from your mistakes**.

Mistakes I made:

Not asking for help when I needed it. Especially in the Spring, I was working myself to death.

Buying used equipment. I don't plan on buying used mowers anymore. With new stuff, you get a warranty, and a little more power at the dealerships.

4. **Marketing**: Word of mouth. That's how I have expanded my lawn care business. Truck/trailer signs are great for getting noticed as well. Yard signs work great as well. Even for small

jobs (ex. bush/hedge trimming job, stick the sign in the yard while you are there, take it with you when you go).

5. **Be professional**. I have shirts, hoodies, windbreakers, all with my logo on the back. I've been walking out of the hardware store and gotten people to ask me about work. I always have jeans on when I'm mowing, shirt always tucked in. Safety equipment: Ear muffs (with the radio of course), glasses, gloves, etc.

You have to show people you are serious, then they will take you seriously. Most people don't even realize I'm a teenager. I normally tell them after we have discussed work and such. Most people are just impressed and willing to support me."

Additional services to offer.

Consider offering stump grinding services this fall to your lawn care customers.

This Fall when you are looking for more services to offer, why not consider offering your lawn care customers, stump grinding services. Why not get on the Gopher Forum and get a free stump grinding flyer template and then hand them out in your area. Try and schedule as many stump grinding services as closely together as you can and then rent a stump grinder for a couple of days.

You could also consider placing an ad in a local paper and mentioning 10% off stump grinding services if you contact us by xx/xx/xx. Or you could use a catchy headline like GET RID OF THAT EYESORE STUMP. Service your lawn care customer's stumps and make some great money to get your through the winter!

If you are unsure about how to price your stump grinding services here is a suggestion from the Gopher Lawn Care Business Forum.

Large stump grinding services range around $150-$300. Small stumps are about $75.

If you are interested in taking these services further you could offer tree removal services. Here are some price guidelines.

Small trees up to about 30-feet high - $125-$450

Medium-sized trees from 30-60 feet tall - $175-$900

Large trees 60-80 feet high - $400-$1,000

Largest Trees 80-100 feet high - $950-$1,400+

How to make more money with your pressure washer.

One of our forum members was very kind to share with us some of the pressure washing marketing material he successfully uses and some of his insights on offering pressure washing as an add on service. I asked him some questions on the topic of marketing and I want to pass the information on to you.

What advice do you have for newer lawn care business owners when it comes to successfully distributing such marketing material? How should one go about using the postcards or door hangers to get the most effective results?

"Just like in real estate…. It's all about location, location, location. In this case, it's list, list, list! Who gets your marketing material is more important than how or what they get.

I don't market to folks that can't afford or shouldn't be hiring out contractors. If they can't afford it, then it is a waste of my efforts. If they shouldn't be affording it, then it too will be a waste because they will want the work cheap.

As for what the marketing material should say…. well, I like promoting what I sell. I stopped selling pressure washing once I found that is was only worth so much. I started selling something more valuable… Time and Convenience! That's why the postcard I mail out doesn't have a mower or pressure washer on it. It has what I propose hiring me will give them… Time to enjoy their free time."

That is a really good point that I think a lot of new lawn care business owners miss. Do you have any advice on how a lawn care business owner can or should determine who can't afford such a service?

"In the past, as long as I was telling the customer about pressure washing, I was getting that look of… "It's just pressure washing, why so much money"… When I started sending a different message to a different mindset client, I noticed more yeses, no matter the price. We went from charging $250 for house pressure washes to $450+ house washes in one season. And started selling more of them at the higher rate. Silly, how a different approach can sell the same pressure washing service for more $$.

As for determining the marketing target, I look for neighborhoods where there is lots of activity. Work vehicles are coming and going. These folks out source this kind of work. I target business owners. Their time is valuable and they also understand us. We have something in common. Hey, a lawyer that is billing $500/hr thinks I am a bargain at $300/hr. Also, don't base your price on YOUR numbers… Base it on THEIR numbers. I sell house washes that would take the typical homeowner a whole weekend to do. I base pricing on that production rate… Not my own. I can clean their home in an hour, but not going to price it at that rate. I'm going to sell them that I am saving them money versus the time it would cost THEM to do it. Hell, even to have the local handyman do it. Not to knock them, but I can wash 5-6 times faster than most of them, but I ain't gonna price it for faster. I'm not gonna stay at the same $50/hr that a lawn/handyman is going to price it at, because I'm faster I'll make $300/hr."

These are great concepts to be considering when you are selling your pressure washing services. In fact you can use these marketing and selling concepts when you sell any of your lawn care business services.

Are you offering lawn mower repair services this fall and winter?

This Fall and Winter when things slow down, have you considered offering lawn mower repair services? It's important to keep yourself busy and meet new potential customers.

You might think, what is the point in offering mower repair and Winterization services? Well first off, you are most likely very fluent in the maintenance of a mower. Most people are not. You will have a great opportunity to reach out and meet new members of your community where you might not normally be able to meet them.

Just because they cut their own lawn doesn't mean they won't call you in the future for other services you offer. The more people you know you, the better your chances are of making a sale.

Here are some services you could offer.

- Change and dispose oil.
- Replace spark plug.
- Clean the under carriage.
- Sharpen and balance blades.
- Spot paint bare metal.
- Change air filter or clean foam filter.

- Check tire inflation.
- Check battery.
- Drain fuel to prepare for Winter.

You could do all these services on site and while you are there, why not ask the customer if there are any other services they could use around their house.

Are seasonal flower beds a profitable upsell?

Lawn care business owners should always be looking for ways to sell more to their current customer base. One idea on how to sell more is by offering seasonal flower beds. Should you consider offering this service? Is it profitable? Would it be worth your while? Or should you subcontract this out and focus on your core competency? Let's take a look.

One of our forum members wrote us and asked "I had a home owners association contact me wanting a quote on their entrance maintenance and then a quote for planting their flower beds up front... I don't know much about seasonal flowers and I was wanting some help as to what type of flowers to suggest for the beds.

I figure a seasonal type bed would look the best for them so there are different blooms as the year goes by, any suggestions would be greatly appreciated!!!

I am going to try and get by one of the local nursery and speak with them before hand also, but the meet is set for 12pm tomorrow and I would like to have a little information to walk in with."

A lawn care business owner responded and said "One of my niche's is flower bed design!! I make a lot of extra money doing so. What I have found with flower beds is that it's a very personal thing! What I might think is lovely, the home owner might hate! Some people love lots of greenery and shrubs…and some may want lots of flowers…some perennials and some annuals. It's all up to the client.

I speak from experience…don't get in over your head doing something that you've never done before. Unless flower bed design is something you're thinking about continuing doing. I would still recommend starting out doing a residential project first though. Especially if you specialize in maintenance. I don't know how your company is set up…or if you have employees..but I've found that even though the income for these projects might seem great…the time and energy you'll spend figuring out how to go the job right will take away from your regular customers. There is a lot more to flowerbeds than…dig a hole and put something pretty in the ground. Spacing…sun light requirements…weather to go with annuals or perennials?? You can definitely figure it all out…but to know it all before your meeting might be pushing it! lol

Have you thought about maybe during your meeting treating it as a consultation?? Getting more info about what your client's wants…and then letting them know you'll get back to them with your plan in a week?? Then you would have time to sub-contract out the flower beds…and you can take the maintenance portion? I wish you all the luck in the world…let us know how it goes!!!!"

Another shared "flower beds are too labor intensive to be

profitable in many cases. Timing, proper soil conditioning, watering, adding nutrients, replacing dead flowers…ugh.

I have always had better results with tree and shrubbery beds instead of flowers. Flowering trees (weeping cherries, etc.) always get applause this time of year.

Know your zone and know what works best in your soil. Be selective in your approach of shrub selection to get coloration through the year. Hollies with heavy berry growth give a nice touch, nandina get colorful in late summer, barberry show red through the summer. Add bulbs for color intensity.

Pick plants that fit with your project. Don't force a plant where it doesn't belong. Think about long term growth…don't plant a tall growing tree under a power line. Learn about landscape design and follow some simple concepts; symmetry, triangular plant spacing, three level display.

One of the hardest parts of landscaping is educating your customer. Go in with a plan and a solid understanding of every plant you plan to install."

I hope this discussion really gets you thinking about whether offering seasonal flower beds is an upsell your lawn care business could easily perform with a good profit margin. It also points out something to think about if you are a new lawn care business owner. You could initially focus on offering this service and market yourself to other mowing businesses in the area. It could be a great niche for you to specialize in.

How your lawn care business can winterize irrigation systems and make money.

Winterizing lawn irrigation systems is a great add on service that is easy to do and can bring you in some good money in the fall. A Gopher Lawn Care Business Forum member wrote and asked how to do this.

"Hi guys I have a question. Do you think a 25 CFM @ 175 PSI, 13 HP Horizontal Air Compressor would be ok to use to blow out residential homes? I got a contract with a realty company with 50 properties. The previous lawn care company did not blow out the systems last year. I have been fixing all of the lawn care customers irrigation systems and mowing their lawns."

A member answered "It should work. I would never use a tow behind though. Remember, DO NOT blow air for more than 2 minutes through the zone. Air compress more than water, and it heats up BIG TIME! You will melt the irrigation pipe if you go crazy with the air."

Another member added "I agree. Make sure you use it no more

than 2 minutes and no higher than 40 psi or you run the risk of damaging the vacuum pressure valve and the solenoid zone valve. Also you will need to have a compressor that will deliver a min 5 cfm @ 40 psi."

Do you have any suggestions on when to market this service?

"Marketing for sprinkler winterization should be started in the Aug - Sept time frame. You can also get on the phone and talk to your current customers about your winterization. You might consider offering a discount for being a mowing client. Also do not forget about those estimates you did during the mowing season that you did not land. Those lawn care estimates are still potential customers for other services. Ask your current clients to spread the word and if a potential customer says no, try to get the last word in i.e. 'well if you know of some one that needs our service please give them my information.'

Second make sure you are ready to go. Check your equipment out good. You can't afford to have a compressor go down, especially if you have 6-7 blow-out for the day. It pays to have a backup compressor."

A third lawn care business owner wrote "I just finished winterizing the irrigation systems of all my customers. I used a large tow behind diesel air compressor. The air line was a 1 inch diameter hose. The air hoses came in 50 ft lengths. The average yard needed two lengths to reach to the blow out bib. The compressor had a gate valve for air control. The bib adapter also had a gate valve. The 100 ft of hose didn't heat up at all.

Costs:

- The compressor rental ended up costing $100 for the compressor for the day.

- $10.00ea for the 50 ft hoses.
- So for $120.00 I rented out a compressor.
- I used about $20.00 in diesel to top off the tank.

It took me about an hour at each job site. So doing 6-7 places in a day and paying approx $140.00 for the rental. You can do the math. I charged each lawn care customer $60.00 - $70.00 per blow out.

Profit:

- (7 customers) x ($70 per customer) = $490
- ($490 gross income) - ($140 expenses) = $350 profit per day."

Spring & Fall home and yard clean up service ideas for your lawn care business.

Anyone who has a house and a yard tends to collect a lot of junk they wish they could just get rid of each year. Sometimes though it's such a pain in the butt to get rid of the stuff, that it just collects.

It's a pain to haul it to the curb. Or the town simply won't pick some stuff up. Our homes & yards become filled with junk.

Why not do this. Create a flyer that promotes a Spring and Fall Home and Yard Cleanup. Hand them out to your neighbors. Get a dumpster delivered to your home and put a banner on it to promote that it's now time to clean up your yard.

Then your neighbors can call you to come over and remove junk from their yard and house they just don't want anymore. You can charge them either by weight or weight and time or time alone. Figure out how much it would cost to get a dumpster delivered and then you can figure how much you need to charge.

This is a very unique service that will really do great things for your neighborhood and endear you to your neighbors. If you do this regularly, your neighbors will look forwards to it. Plus it can make you money in the Fall and early Spring.

Getting started offering gutter cleaning services.

Offering gutter cleaning, at first can appear to be a daunting challenge, but don't let this stop you from making money on a service many others won't do. This is a great way to bring in extra income during the fall that can help your lawn care business when your mowing services slow down. One of our Gopher Lawn Care Business Forum members recently started his lawn care business and asked "this year is my first year in business and it has been a learning process for me. I need some help with something. In the fall other than racking leaves what else is there to do? I know a little about cleaning gutters but all I know to do is climb on a ladder and pull out the leaves. What else do I need to clean a gutter other than a ladder? Keep in mind that I'm on a low-budget. Also I live on the east coast and I don't know anything about charging for fall-clean ups so some tips on that would also be great."

A lawn care business owner responded "I have found that the best way to clean out gutters is with a blower….Back pack preferred.

Charging for a leaf clean-up can be tough. Customers love to try and get the job done at a very cheap price. However, you have to think about several things when you do the estimate.

1. Are all the leaves off the trees?

2. How large is the property?

3. Do they want you to rid them or blow them into the woods?

4. How long is it going to take to complete the work?

There are many options out there and leaf clean-up is a lot of work. So, charge by the hour for one and charge extra if they want you to take it away."

Another member shared "Cleaning gutters is definitely big business for the Fall months. Cleaning gutters can be dangerous though so be sure to follow all safety regulations including fall protection.

Don't stop at simply cleaning the gutters though. Offer a free inspection.

   * If you find loose fasteners you can replace them.
   * If there is a leak at a joint, offer to repair it.
   * You can also offer to install gutter leaf guards.

The list is endless. You can make tons of money between now and the end of the year if you price it right."

A third member said "do you have a gas powered blower? Electric will work (if you have tons of cord) But the fastest way is to just get up on the roof and blow them out of the gutter. If you have a powerful gas blower be careful on the trigger as 283 mph wind from a gas blower will tear off the gutters. Then once you have the gutters cleaned out treat the job like any other kind of leaf removal service. If you don't have a blower I would suggest biting the bullet and buying a cheaper gas powered one. It will pay itself off in the fall very fast. I guarantee!"

Lastly a final viewpoint "my experience has shown me that the fastest way to 'properly' clean out the gutters is to get up on a ladder and clean them by hand. I have used the blower attachments and they make a mess like no other. Especially if the gutters are wet. You'll find yourself cleaning off the roof, house, windows and yourself.

I charge $1.00 per linear foot with a minimum charge of $55.00. Depending on your costs, overhead, dumping fees, etc...your price will differ."

I hope this discussion helps get you on the right track and gets you excited to offer an additional service in the Fall. Remember each season presents you with great ways to make more money. You don't have to simply focus on cutting lawns.

How to get started offering holiday decoration and lighting services.

The winter months can be a tough time for a lawn care business. More and more lawn care businesses are getting into offering outdoor holiday lighting and decoration services to help them get through the slow times. Those who have experimented with it seem to be pretty happy with the results but how do you get started in offering these services?

One of our forum members asked "I'm just getting started in offering holiday decoration services and I'm really not sure how to go about bidding on hanging lights. I put a nice ad in my local newspaper and have been receiving responses. My going rate for lawn care is $60/hourly. Also the holiday lighting estimates will be for both putting up and taking the lights down. I will be using the customers lights. Should I possibly ask if I need to supply the product? I have a few customers already calling and I procrastinated. If someone could help me that would be awesome. Thanks."

Since this is your first time doing this, why not decorate your house with some lights and figure out how long it takes you to do some standard lighting, such as running lights across the roof line. Figure out how long it takes by the linear foot. This should then help you measure other homes and get an idea how long the job will be.

Then if you are going to be taking them down as well, you will need to double that fee. Why not try and keep your hourly rate of $60 the same in your bids.

If you want to offer your own lights, why not consider figuring out how much lights are costing and buy them as needed. Charge the customer for the lights and then you will be able to take them down and reuse them next year as well. You could consider charging double the cost of the lights.

A forum member added "I charge by the hour. I sell the clients the lights or they buy lights themselves. I put them up and take them down. When I take them down, I put them in some big Tupperware containers and put them in their garage. I know I could get a lot more because I've heard of guys doing a $1,000 a house and being very basic. I've been charging like $300 for a better job. It's still new to me though. I have looked at some of the "holiday lighting whole sellers" and they seem to be the same as a box store, so I just purchase them locally. If the client owns the lights then you explain that every year they will more than likely have to buy a few new sets because they go out. Plus if they want to expand on it they can do so a few pieces at a time.

It usually takes me until lunch for $150 and $150 to take them down which takes less time. You can make a lot more but once again I am new to this and am figuring out my costs."

Another member added "I installed 6 strings of 50 LEDS with a light clip for every light on a two story house. I charged by the hour and supplied the lights. It was a simple light around the roof job. The cost was $20 per box of lights and $5 dollars per box of 100 clips. It took 5.5 to 6 hrs to install. I charged $380.00."

Keep experimenting with offering holiday lighting and decoration services. Try to increase your sale price with each customer as you go. From the discussions I have had with other lawn care business who have done this for a few years, they try and shoot for $750 to $1,000 per house. This includes installing the decorations and taking them down. You can use your own decorations or use the customers. Try both ways and see which works best for you. I have also included some free postcard and door hanger design templates on the forum you can use to market this service.

Out of lawn care and into dog waste disposal.

Starting a lawn care business and getting a bunch of commercial grade equipment can be quite expensive. One the Gopher Lawn Care Business Forum members wrote and shared with us how he got out of offering lawn care and now specializes in dog waste disposal. He wrote "I have shut down the lawn mowing and have been pushing the poop scooping business and I am pleased with the results."

Can you tell us a little about why you decided to go with the dog waste removal business and shut down your lawn care business?

"Keep in mind that this is my extra money job for now. I am only doing this part time as I work a full time job as well. At first I was kind of hesitant to offer this service for the obvious messy reasons, but aside from the "I scoop poop" factor when talking to people it's really not bad. Since I work nights at my full time job, I'm used to really long hours in the winter with the snow plowing I do. I have been mowing lawns for 2 years using my 22" mower and it wasn't horrible, but it was slow going.

I did well and had reached the point where if I were going to add customers I HAD to get a large walk behind or zero turn and a trailer. I kept thinking this is gonna cost me 4 to 6 grand. Most of my lawns are $30 dollar lawns which is not bad. I would spend 45 minutes to an hour there and was satisfied with the income. Then I really started looking at the poop scooping business. The cost for the basic equipment is $30. I can spend more if I want but even if I went hog wild and bought everything I want it still wouldn't be too much. Here is what I got so far:

- Used pickup truck like a ford ranger $5,000
- Decals $300
- Laptop $500 for in the truck
- Printer $60 for in the truck
- Water tank (for cleaning equipment) $100
- Scoop $15
- Rake $6
- Shirts and other misc stuff $300

I can do without most of this stuff for now and for 10 minutes work I make $15. I did an initial cleaning last week and for 1hr 45min made $90 (for initials I charge $30 minimum for 2 gallons of dog waste, then $15 for each additional 2 gallons. I use a 5 gallon paint bucket and I call that 4 gallons so the customers really gets a break. So far so good."

I think this is a fascinating look at how there are so many different businesses out there you can get involved in! Some have a higher barrier of entry than others. It's nice to know you can get your dog waste removal business started for the price of a bucket and a shovel! Experiment offering this service and you too may find yourself getting out of the lawn care field or making this a new upsell service.

Sample marketing letters.

Fall lawn care leaf cleanup letter also used for gutter cleaning.

One of our forum members shared with us this fall leaf clean up letter. Before Fall comes along, why not send out this letter in your invoices to your lawn care customers. Ask them how you should handle their leaf clean up and also offer other additional Fall services like gutter cleaning.

A lawn care business owner suggested when bidding out your gutter cleaning, to charge $60 per hour. This should help you when you are estimating your jobs.

Here is another way, a forum member shared, to bid on gutter cleaning jobs. He said "You're leaving money on the table doing it by the hour.

If you are called to a residential property just for gutter clean out you should be charging by the foot and it should include down spout flushing. $1 a ft and if it's 2 story it should be a little extra for the height. ALWAYS PRACTICE SAFETY WHEN WORKING OFF LADDERS AND ON ROOFS. AN INJURY CAN TAKE YOU OUT OF THE GAME COMPLETELY, COSTING YOU MORE THAN MONEY.

If your doing a fall clean up, (leaf clean up and removal) gutter clean out should be included. Plant beds are not extra either, they are a part of the lawn.

These are common practices with-in my area."

I thought this was very interesting! So I asked, when you give a bid for a fall yard cleanup, do you include a line item that shows gutter cleaning and a price for that? Do you include another line item for plant beds? Or are all these included into one price and it isn't broken down at all?

He said "This is what I include. We here by propose to; clear all lawn and plant bed ares of leaves to the best of our ability. Clean and flush all gutters and down spouts as follows,

Fall Lawn Clean Up $X.XX
(All lawn and plant bed areas)

Gutter Clean Out $X.XX
(Cleaning and flushing all gutter & down spouts)

Total Due $X.XX

If the customer balks at the gutter charges then explain to them the importance of having them cleaned out. Most will go for it."

Here is a sample letter you could include in your invoices to help sell this service.

Dear Valued Customer,

With Fall nearly upon us, and assuming you have trees in or near your yard, leaves will soon be falling and covering your lawn.

Since Fall clean-up are not included in our basic service, we need to find out how you would like to deal with leave removal.

We can either:

1. Mow as usual, mulching the leaves back into the lawn, allowing them to break down naturally at no additional charge or;

2. Rake, bag and dispose of the leaves.

If you wish to have the leaves removed, we will be happy to provide you with a free quote.

Don't forget to ask about our additional services.

1. Gutter Cleaning
2. Hedge Trimming
3. Flower Bed Weeding
4. Power Washing
5. Brush Removal
6. Bush Hogging
7. Storm Cleanup

If you need a home or lawn service that's not listed, give us a call.

As always, thank you so much for your business and please call us at any time for any reason.

Sincerely,

Your Name

Owner

3 month before and after lawn care customer retention letter sample.

One important thing to remember is that most lawn care customers who are going to cancel service will cancel it shortly after signing up with you. From a post on the Gopher Forum a member who studied this said "When researching our cancellation history I found that most of the canceled lawn care accounts had been canceled within the first 3-4 months. If they had been more informed from the beginning, maybe we could have saved the sale."

So if we know that most customers who cancel, tend to cancel early on in the service, due to buyers remorse or a feeling of guilt from spending money on lawn service, why not stop that problem before it happens. Give the customer a good reason why they should keep having you service their yard. Show them the value they are receiving.

One way to do this would be to create a before and after customer letter that focused on a specific problem you were able to resolve. How can you do this?

- When you first sign up a new customer, take some photos of problem areas on their property.
- Within 3 months, try to resolve at least one of those specific problems and take photos of how the property looks afterwards.
- Then send a letter to the customer that shows them how you are working to resolve issues with their lawn and show how you were able to achieve it on this specific section.
- Maybe put this letter in with your 3rd month invoice or send it separately with a special envelope that says 3 month lawn status on the back.
- Ultimately the customer will feel they are receiving value and will want to continue using your lawn care service.

Here is a lawn care customer template to help you get started with this.

Dear Customer,

3 Month Lawn Care Update.

I wanted to take a moment and thank you for choosing Joe's Lawn Service to provide you with the best lawn care available. Over these past few months I have been hard at work resolving issues your lawn was struggling with.

I have included a before and after picture of one particular troubled lawn spot that has been resolved. You can see the brown spots on the before picture and a few months later in the same area, the spots are now gone. The reason this spot was occurring was due to a brown spot fungus. Such a fungus will not go away by itself and needed to be treated.

It is my privilege to work for you and help you create that perfect lawn. If you find other problems about your yard you want address, don't hesitate to contact me through email or call my cell phone.

Regards,
Your Name

Lawn care business commercial property bid cover letter sample.

When your lawn care business is submitting a bid for commercial property maintenance, consider including this bid cover letter sample. It's a great way to look professional and improve your chances at winning the lawn care bid.

Mr. Smith
123 Main St
Anytown, USA 90210
(800) 123-4567

RE: Weekly Lawn Maintenance

Dear Mr. Smith,

Thank you for inviting XXXX Lawn Care the opportunity to submit this proposal to provide you with lawn care services for your property located in CITY, STATE.

The pricing bid for this property is outlined on the enclosed quotation sheet. The cost is based on weekly mowing, trimming, edging, and blowing down of all hard surfaces. Five (5) premium fertilizing applications and a spring core aerating. If you find any of this information to be in question please give me a call at xxx-xxxx.

Again, thank you for the opportunity to submit this proposal. We are excited to establish this new business relationship. We are looking forward to doing business with you this year and we are confident you will be extremely pleased with our services.

Sincerely,

Your Name
Owner

End of lawn care season customer letter sample.

When the lawn mowing season comes to a close you might want to consider sending your customers this end of the season lawn care letter. This is a great way to reach out to your lawn care customers and say thank you.

December 1, 20XX

Homeowner
10 Any Street
Your city, State 90210

Dear Customer,

I would like to thank you again for choosing Joe Smith Landscaping for your lawn needs. We hope you were more then satisfied with our performance. This season is coming to a close and this will be the last billing for the year. If you need any last minute services before winter sets in, feel free to contact us. We will be sending out a letter in March to welcome you back to the new season. Until then, we hope you and your family will have a safe and happy winter.

Sincerely,

Joe Smith
888-555-9487
Email: joe@gopherforum.com
Web: www.gopherforum.com

Snow plow and property maintenance letter.

If you are looking to provide snow plowing services or property management services to home owners in your area, here is a great sample letter you can send out in fall to line up potential customers. One of the Gopher Lawn Care Business Forum members wrote "I provide property care taking and snow removal service during the non lawn season. Here is a letter I sent out to over 200 homeowners. Most of the homeowners don't permanently live here, but have a second home here. Out of those 200 letters, I received 8 responses and ended up getting 4 snow plowing jobs, one property care taking job, and a lawn contract for next year."

Dear Homeowner,

Please allow me to introduce myself to you. My name is Joe, and I have lived in Your Town, since this Month of this Year. During much of that time I have operated my own property management company.

Winter in (Your Town, Your State) is just around the corner. One thing that comes with winter is snow. It is not a question of whether or not we will receive snow, but more a question of how much. With snow on the way, it is also a question as to who will keep your property cleared of that snow.

There is nothing like the falling of fresh snow. It seems to brighten up the world and give it a sense of freshness. It also means it is time to get to work and clean up the driveway and the sidewalks. It's not always an easy task and not always a task that one can accomplish for several reasons, such as health, time or your not being here to take care of it.

Snow in the driveway should never be ignored. It is important to have a clean, snow free driveway. A snow filled driveway is like having a sign on your home saying Vacancy.

Added security to your home can start with something as simple as plowing the driveway and this service can be added to our weekly property inspections.

Along with clearing snow, I provide weekly house checks and inspections for a number of homes in the area. Your home can be placed on our schedule to be checked each week for problems ranging from water leaks, broken windows, roof leaks and any other problems which may arise in your absence.

We offer a service to take care of your property when you are not here to do so. Among those services are things as simple as watering your house plants and starting your vehicle while checking your home.

We are fully insured and have a list of references which can be viewed on our website. You will see that we are dedicated to our job and our clients and treat every property as though it was our own.

Contact (Your Lawn Care Services) to take care of your property. We will gladly put you on a schedule to have your property cleared of snow and your unoccupied home checked each week.

Sincerely,

Your Name

Lawn Care Business Customer Referral letter sample.

If you are looking to increase your lawn care customer base, a great way to do it is by increasing your referrals. How do you increase your referrals? You can start by simply asking your current customers to help you out with a letter. You would be amazed at how your current customer base would be willing to help you out if they only knew you wanted them to do it. Here is a sample letter you can edit to fit your specific needs. One thing to keep in mind before you send out this letter is do not send it with an invoice. Your customers probably won't be in the mood to help you when they are writing a check. Instead, pick another time during the month to do this and include a few business cards in the letter.

Homeowner
1 Your Street
Your Town, State Zip

Dear Homeowner,

I would like to take a moment to thank you for helping us grow last year. We really appreciate you helping "spread the word" about our company and services we provide.

As we are entering the spring of this new year we would really appreciate your continued support. If you know of anyone, friends, family or neighbors, who are in need of the services we provide, please consider suggesting us. We have included a few business cards you can hand to them.

In return for your referral of any job totaling $100 or more to a new customer, we will provide you with any one choice of the following services: one cubic yard of double ground hardwood mulch, a turf fertilizer application, or one free mow.

Thank you again for your support of our company. We look forwards to seeing you this spring.

Should you require any new services this year, or if you have any questions, please do not hesitate to contact me.

Sincerely,

Your Contact Information

A landscaping and lawn care debt collection letter that works.

Do you have a customer or customers who tell you repeatedly the check is in the mail? Maybe they have even go so far as to tell you they aren't going to pay you. One of our Gopher Lawn Care Business Forum members had to deal with this issue until she sent out a letter that got her dead beat lawn care customer to pay up.

She wrote and said she was dealing with two deadbeat customer situations. This is how she dealt with the situation. "First, I called the Small Claims Court in my County and gathered information on starting a small court claim. I found out how much to file, how much for the Sheriff to serve papers, etc. Then, I gathered my information regarding my deadbeat client; like the dates we performed lawn & garden maintenance and filled in the blanks. I wrote a letter to the dead beat customer and in it I stressed she had 5 days after the receipt of the letter to settle her bill. If not, then I will file a claim against her for theft of services.

I went to the post office and sent the letter registered mail. Three days later, I received her payment in full. I ran to the bank and deposited the check hoping she didn't put a stop payment on it! Accompanying her check was a little nasty note stating that she was the one who fired us, but that doesn't excuse her nonpayment.

Here's the lawn care business debt collection letter format that I used. I removed the personal information so others who use it can just fill in the blanks appropriately."

Dear deadbeat:

You had hired ABC Lawn Care Company on (insert date) to perform garden maintenance at 3 week intervals, starting on this day. At the same time, you hired us for lawn maintenance at an agreed price of $$, starting this day. Since then, I've performed garden maintenance per our contract on this day and lawn maintenance was performed on the following dates. Payment terms per our contract are due upon completion. Payments for the services listed above are now due immediately. Despite several phone calls to you to collect payment, you have stated on 3 separate occasions that your payment is in the mail. Since I have not received payment to date, your services were terminated by ABC Lawn Care Company on said date, due to theft of services.

As per our contract, I am requesting to be paid $$$ for our services.

If I do not hear from you within 5 days from the receipt of this letter, then I will file a petition with small claims court in Your County.

I look forward to working with you toward a resolution of this matter.

Very truly,

Your Name

What to include in your hand written thank you card?

Each year you should consider dropping off a hand written thank you card to your lawn care customers. You don't have to do them all at once. Just break down your lawn care customer list and do them step by step. This is a great way to build up your lawn care business referrals.

What should you include in your hand written thank you card? How about something like this.

Dear Customer,

Thank you for your business. I really appreciate it. Keep in mind if you need to get in touch with me for any reason, please call. Also if you could, please pass on a few of my business cards to anyone you know who might need my services. I would be thankful for any referrals you could send my way.

Sincerely,
Joe

Don't forget to include three business cards along with the thank you card.

Lawn care business press release idea.

In general I don't think lawn care business owners utilize press releases as much as they should. The media, especially the local media, is always looking for a news story. Why not give them one? What does it cost to offer them a news idea? Nothing more than a little time to write up a press release and send it out to the local press.

Now I know that can be a little difficult and perhaps daunting of a challenge so I thought it would be a great experiment to put together a sample press release article idea that you could use and change the names in it and then send out to your local press. Then any lawn care business owner who used this idea and got an article written about them, could get onto the Gopher Forum and tell us about how it happened and their experience. Plus they could tell us what kind of results came from being spotlighted in the local media.

Title: Local resident offers his own economic stimulus plan.

With our economy in a downward spiral and the federal

government offering up what seems to be a new economic recovery plan every week, local resident John Smith, has an answer on how to fix this mess we are in.

In one word, he summed up his plan. "Jobs. We need to create jobs." We can no longer rely on our current employer to protect us in an economic downturn. Businesses are going belly up all over the place. It's our duty to harness our energy and creativity and create jobs."

John Smith is the owner of Smith's Lawn Care which has operated in town for the past X years. "If we each take a moment and think about what our skill set is, we could create a business and create jobs, today! Right now! We shouldn't be looking to the government to hand us out an unemployment check. We need to create jobs and hand out a paycheck. We need to make our township, county, state and country the best it can be by creating.

Each one of us can do something another person needs. Can you babysit? Can you cook? Can you cut lawns? Can you paint a house? Can you build a website. Figure out what you can do and do it. Then hire someone to help."

With this Spring just around the corner, John plans on hiring local residents to help perform lawn care and landscaping services. "If we each do a little, together we can do a lot."

President John F. Kennedy's inaugural address concluded with this famous line. "And so, my fellow Americans, ask not what your country can do for you; ask what you can do for your country." Now more than ever we need to do for our country. We need to fix this economic situation. We have the power to fix this situation and we will fix it if each one of us stands up, takes a step forward and reaches out to others to help them.

Create jobs!

Now you can either send this to your local paper as a press release to get them to call you and interview you or you can send this in as a letter to the editor. Take the text, change it around to fit your specific situation and send it in! It's free advertising and it's a positive message that will reflect positively on you and your business.

Try it out and let me know how it works.

Promoting your lawn care business through local schools.

I am so impressed with the creative marketing ideas that come through the Gopher Lawn Care Business Forum. One of our friends shared with us his idea to market his lawn care business through local schools and teach kids some useful information along the way.

He posted a letter he is planning on sending to the local school principals and I am going to include it here along with my view on what else you could do.

He wrote "I'm emailing principals of schools in my area. I hope this works. This is a sample of the letter.

Dear Mr/Mrs _____ of _____ School

I am the owner of Joe's Lawn Service here in Your Town.

I came up with a fun & creative project that all students can take part in.

My plan would be to explain to the students about the complexities of starting their own business.
Example:

The Plan (is it possible? is it needed?)
The Budget (when can i start?)
The Requirements (what is needed)
Marketing (who/what/when/where/why)
Competition (how to lead, how to gain without lowering your service costs, etc)

After the above, I would ask of them to take a Joe's Lawn Service flyer & business card home with them.

If the household owners of the students are interested in hiring my lawn care service, each student will gain $20.00 for their support, & the homeroom class of the students will receive the required amount of Pizza.

I would encourage students to work hard & focus while in class, letting them know & to understand the importance of putting in the hard work while the opportunity is given to them. I would explain the possible outcome of people who have refused to take school seriously, & how they are currently struggling.

I would love to explain to the students the difference of having a job vs having a career, & the cost of living.

I believe most students don't know about the frightening truth of what their life will become once they are on their own, without someone to take care of them. I also believe once the students get an idea, it will give them a goal to achieve.

Thank you for your time,

Joe"

Now I thought this was a fantastic idea which you could take in many different ways. I am thinking you might get a better response if you don't make it too commercial. I love everything commercial, but with schools and kids, they may be a little picky on this. I would probably take out the section about the business flyer and the pizza.

Instead of saying that, you could do other things. Like maybe come up with a coloring book sheet that allowed the students to color in a mower or maybe an outline of what you talked about.

You could also hand out promotional magnets or tshirts or stuff kids would like. The magnets could promote mower safety and list 5 safety points and at the bottom it could have your business name and number. They could be handed out at the end of the seminar to let the kids hang their coloring page up on their refrigerator.

You could also talk about outdoor power equipment safety and give a hand out on the dangers of the equipment.

Create a coloring page you could hand out to the kids and get them into the activity of coloring in the page as well as writing what safety equipment should be worn while mowing a lawn.

Experiment with this topic and see what you can come up with. If you end up offering this seminar, make you take pictures and send them to your local newspaper to get even more publicity.

Marketing discussion & ideas.

Lawn care marketing idea in a cup!

If you are looking for a way to stand out when you do your lawn care estimates, why not do what our Gopher Forum members does when he visits a home to do a lawn care estimate.

He wrote "Every time I do an estimate… the estimate sheet, brochure and biz card go in a plastic cup. The cup I use is silk screened to display my logo and business contact information and placed on the door step. I feel most people won't throw it away, so the shelf life of the cup is worth it. You could do this with can coolies as well but they are almost 3 times the cost. I can get cups for about 50 cents a piece depending on the quantity."

How often when you do estimates is someone home? Do you hand the cup to a lot of people when they are home or are most out during the day and just want you to come by and leave an estimate?

What kind of response have you gotten to using the cup? Has it improved your estimate acceptance rate?

He responded "I do lot's of estimates, at least 100+ in the Spring time alone. Usually no one is home, so I leave the cup, estimate, brochure, etc. On the front porch. I can't say if it gets a better response or not, but I feel with the right materials it makes you look more professional and not like some fly by night company."

This is also a great way to promote your lawn care business by going door to door and leaving a flyer in the cup as well. Maybe even include a pen. So consider these ideas next time you are looking for a way to stand out.

Lawn care marketing direct mail response rates.

Most lawn care business owners experiment with direct mail for their lawn care marketing and often wonder what kind of response rate they should be seeing.

A Gopher Forum member sent out mailings for his lawn care business and asked this question.

He said "I've sent 475 color stump removal promotion flyers on Wednesday and I only received 1 estimate so far. I've seen most of my flyers in the garbage can at the post office. Does this mean people are tired of flyers?"

Another lawn care business owner responded by saying "No that is actually a reasonable response from 475 flyers.

A good industry standard for direct mail is a 1-2% response rate. But I'll tell you it's been a long time since I've seen a 1% response from any of my mailings. So at 1% you should have gotten about 4.75 calls. That might seem a little low…

However… You are marketing a service that is VERY unique. I don't know how it is in your area, but in mine, there just are not that many stumps that need to be ground down. For example if you did a flyer for "grass cutting" let's say, you know that just about everyone who sees your flyer, (or if you distribute them you can make sure) has a lawn. You don't know if everyone, who saw your flyer, has a stump that needs ground down. So you have shrunk your market. The same would be true if you marketed dog fence installation. If you mailed to every home in a neighborhood, you have no idea who has a dog or not. Even though your flyer has other services on it, the only thing that customers see is the "stump grinding" headline at the top.

Since customers only look at these things for a split second, they are not seeing anything else but the main selling point. If they are interested in that, they might look at your other services, but not unless they want the main service your offering on the flyer. Does that make sense?

So I say if you got one from 475 that is a good response. I think many people don't realize how many flyers, postcards, door hangers, or whatever… it really takes to really get a large number of sales.

Don't get frustrated, keep putting them out!!!"

Lawn care business flyer response rates.

Have you been handing out flyers, trying to promote your Spring lawn care business services and not getting the response you thought you would be getting? There could be many reasons why this happens. Could it be your headline? Or maybe even your offer? Let's look into this.

A lawn care business owner wrote us and said "I've put out approximately 1,500 flyers and have only had 1, maybe 2 calls. I'm offering a month free with an annual agreement and have put a list of all the things we do on the flyer. What is going on?"

Another business owner replied "WOW!! A month free?!?!?! That's crazy that people aren't calling and two that you would offer that! LOL

Keep your head up the business will come!! I normally get 1% to 2% call backs on flyers. I think that's the norm. My only suggestion would be this…and it might sound crazy so hang in there with me.

If it seems that most people are only getting a 1% to 2% call back on fliers…maybe you should put out less flyers at a time BUT put them out more often. I started putting flyers out the middle of Jan and I went out 4 times (once each weekend). I put out between 200 and 300 fliers each time (about a large subdivision worth) but I got about 1 to 2 calls each time. All that said I got 9 customers from that, and I only put out around 1,000 fliers. I'm up to 13 customers so far the rest I got from referrals.

I am also participating in a Women's Conference here where I live. It's a sold out event and there will be 300 people there and about 20 vendors. So I've been prepping for that. Since the majority of the guests will be women at the conference I had gift certificates printed good for one lawn service. I figured that would be a good gift to give their husbands. Father's day is coming up…or even themselves…a lot of servicemen from my area are deployed right now so that means no husband to cut the yard. I put the price of $45 on the flyer and will have one displayed at the table…that gives me a little wiggle room…just in case I may need to take 10% off."

A business owner said "I'm distributing about 2,000 fliers a week. There are so many neighborhoods where I am at that even at the rate, I won't be able to get everyone in my coverage area. Interestingly enough, my only new business lately has come from a yard sign I placed at a busy off-ramp on a major highway coming out of my area. Maybe give that a shot too!

I hit each house once. It's just not physically possible to hit a house a second or third time with the amount of flyers I put out alone. Although, I've been thinking about hiring someone to also help me distribute them out. The only problem with that is all my flyers have different prices on them. I put them accordingly on houses which I would charge that specific amount."

Another suggested "you can't just sit there at the phone waiting for people to call. I've got people that called me last summer to do a fall cleanup and they originally had my 1st flyer from when I started my business 3 years ago! They held onto the flyer for that long! Some people/customers actually take your flyer and think about it."

A fourth member shared "Here is your solution . . .

   1. Stop advertising price, you could be scaring potential customers away that you could up sell to.
   2. Multiple exposures are the only way to do direct mailing.
   3. Example for number two - Husband gets my pressure washing flyer and says ah yes the house is dirty. The door bell rings, he gets distracted and he sits the flyer down. He comes back to the couch and looks for the ad? Oh well let's see whats on tv.
   4.While at the door the wife comes through cleaning and in the trash your flyer goes BYE BYE
   5. Next week he gets another flyer from me. "Oh that's the company I needed to clean my house *ring ring* "Thank you for calling ABC Power Washing and Lawn Care how can I make your life easier?"
   6. The rest is history!!!!

MULTIPLE EXPOSURE IS THE ONLY WAY TO GO TRUST ME . . .. Find a nice little mailing list of local potential customer addresses. You can go door 2 door as well. Shoot for around 1k and mail the hell out of them.

PLEASE TAKE THIS ADVICE IT WORKS!!!!!

If you don't believe me do an internet search for 'direct mail marketing' and read some articles they will all say you need to do 4 -7 mailings to get full results."

Ultimately all these responses really seemed to help the lawn care business owner who asked the question that started this discussion and he said "thanks for the advice! I've been thinking for weeks now whether or not to include a price on my flyer. Generally, I post flyers out at night; I rarely ever get a good view of the backyard, so I just estimate or "guesstimate" in my case.

I created a new flyer with a free template that I found on The Gopher Forum. There are 2 on a page, so I get 150 printed out, which, when cut in half, gives me 300 flyers. The print place will cut them in half for an extra 2 bucks."

3,500 lawn care business postcards mailed and how many results?

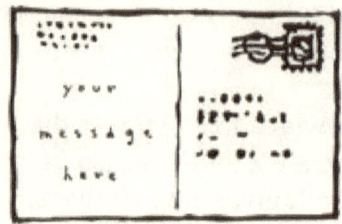

Have you ever sent out quite a bit of lawn care marketing material and gotten back lack luster results or no results at all? It happens. What is really difficult about this is if you are just starting out and you spend a lot of money on marketing and then get nothing in return, you might feel like giving up. If this happens to your lawn care business, don't give up. Marketing is like fishing. You never know when it's going to catch you something. Let's take a look at a story from the Gopher Lawn Care Business Forum.

One of our members wrote "I wanted to send out postcards to promote my lawn care business and what I did first was ask my current clients in my area if they read ad mail? Their response was sometimes "if it catches my eye" and "if it is printed on professional cards." I asked about flyers and the majority said they do not read flyers. If printed on a color photocopy paper, it's used as kindling to start a fire. So the message to me was clear.

I hired a local marketing company, told them what I wanted, they came back with 3 designs. I went back to my clients and asked them to choose. I also asked people at the local market which one they liked. All but one selected the same card. I had 10,000 printed.

I then had it mailed into very specific areas of the city. What we call the South End, a very rich area where for the most part, home owners hire someone to do all the property maintenance for them to keep up with the neighbors. 80% of my sales are attributed to this local area.

The message of this specific post card was our organic products, professional lawn care and clean ups. The card is very sharp. I mailed 3,500 last Thursday, not one call or email has been generated.

Two weeks ago I ran a very simple short ad in a local newspaper, it cost me $18.50, it's drive was mini excavation, I received over twenty grand in contracts and am still receiving calls.

So I guess there is a lesson to be learned. I am a bit shocked at no response at all. I know this area well and the card really should have sparked some attention.

I ask every caller or email, how did you hear about us, 97% is newspaper, 3% search engine. I am not including word of mouth. I also picked up three jobs from people who saw one of my trucks and wrote the number down.

So I will give it one more shot and send 5,000 into the upper middle class area and see what happens, it is a very expensive way to get the name out, even if I had one call…..

I was curious about why this happened so what I did this evening was to write a large number of clients asking if they received our lawn care card. Those in the area I sent it to did indeed get them so I can now rule out the question of if they were delivered or not."

Another forum member shared his views on newspaper ads. He

said post cards and ad packs are usually intercepted by the wife who considers the lawn, the 'duty' of the man of the house and promptly discards it. I don't think postcards are worthwhile.

I also ran a block ad in our local paper in the services section. It cost me $120.00 a quarter (13 weeks). I started the ad last week (it comes out every Monday and is home delivered) and so far I have received 61 calls and my website is getting 35-40 hits a day. I wanted to get 50 new accounts this year and as of today I have gotten 41. I gave 11 estimates today and have 10 set for tomorrow.

I think newspaper ads make you look more 'real' to the customers."

Very fascinating information to consider when you are looking into marketing your lawn care business. What works in one area may not work in another but one thing is for sure. Paying more money on your lawn care marketing does not guarantee it will work better.

How one lawn care business owner is attracting more customers.

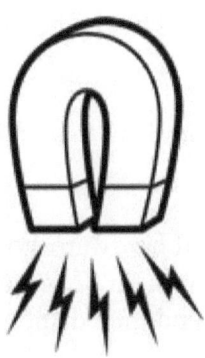

Sometimes the difference between success and failure can be so slight we just don't know when we are close to that line. Many times entrepreneurs can walk within inches of success but give up before crossing over. Recently one of the Gopher Lawn Care Business Forum members got on and posted on how he was having a great day. We are very lucky that he shared with us what he has been doing to improve the awareness of his lawn care business. Taking the small steps here and there as he has can potentially take your lawn care business onto a successful path.

He wrote "I had a great day, today!

I did 3 small lawns, gave 10 estimates and got 4 of them. When I got home, I had 10 phone calls to return and 11 emails replies for Free Estimates from my website (not counting the duplicates).

A happy vent for a change."

That is fantastic news! What kinds of things have you been doing with your lawn care business to see such a positive response to your business?

"I added a blog to my lawn care business website to improve my search engine ranking. I now hold Google positions 1-5 for lawn care service in my area.

I am the only lawn care company that is licensed and insured in my area.

I made a deal with the local hardware store which has helped a lot. I buy my supplies from them (that they carry), rent my equipment when needed, and they display my lawn care fliers in their store.

When canvasing neighborhoods I leave a magnet ad. I either hand it to them or if no one's home I stick it on their metal door if they have one or on the doorknob it they don't. Flyers they just throw away, but the magnet goes on their refrigerator."

If you are looking to push your lawn care business forward, try some or all of these suggestions and you too might start finding yourself having great days as well!

$10 off lawn care customer coupon marketing idea.

What if, instead of lawn care business cards, you had coupons printed up that were the size of dollar bills. You could hold them in your wallet and when you handed them to people, they could keep it in their wallet as well.

You could hand these out to current customers to give to their friends or to people you just meet around town.

You could add in a few conditions like they can not be combined and maybe have an expiration date, but I think it would sure beat just getting a business card. This is something, as a potential customer, you could use!

Maybe you could make these coupons valued at $10 or even experiment with $20.

See how they work out. You could have your wife or husband give these out too. Maybe even your employees or your kids! Heck give your entire extended family some to hand out. Get everyone into the act of promoting your lawn care business.

One of our forum members wrote "I am going to try a few for pressure washing and offer a discount or free mowing service to build up my referrals."

Free mowing special offer. One week only, yard sign.

When you drive around town, I am sure you see plenty of realty sign. Realtors can be quite creative in their marketing and we can learn a lot from them. What if you wanted to build out your lawn care route more and wanted to get more customers in the area where you have current customers. This would potentially make your routes tighter by having multiple customers living on the same block.

How can you do this? Well what if you took a yard sign and added a "please take one" box on the side of it that said Free mowing offer. This week only. You could put this sign in a customer's yard and leave it up for a week. Put a bunch of flyers in it that made a real enticing offer like "spend quality time on the weekends with your family, not with your lawn mower. For one week only we are offering a buy one get one free trial of our lawn care service."

If you call us today, we will perform one free lawn cutting when you buy one.

It's a great way to try us out and see how easy it is to take back your weekends. Remember this great offer is only available this week so call today.

I bet you will get neighbors walking or driving by to stop and see what this Free offer is.

Then the following week, put the sign at another customers house and switch it through each customer each week.

What would be great too, is if you included a clause in your lawn care contract that would allow you to put a promotional sign in your customers lawn for 1 week a year.

A Gopher Forum member wrote "Obviously in some neighborhoods it won't work, mostly because it's not allowed. I bet it could be extremely effective in some neighborhoods though. The sign and flyer box should be relatively cheap, so you really wouldn't be out much to at least test it.

For those neighborhood's that don't allow yard signs, I'd send every house on your customer's street a postcard after every service visit presenting the offer. It's not the same as the yard sign, and it costs a little bit more, but at least this way you're guaranteed to get your sales message delivered instead of depending on the prospect to pull the flyer out of the box!"

How to get lawn care & yard work on foreclosed homes.

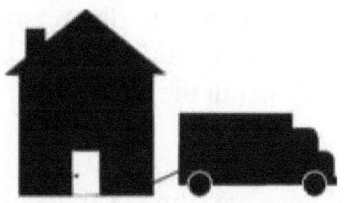

With the economy slowing, more and more homes are being foreclosed upon. As they sit uninhabited, someone has to maintain them or they will fall into disrepair. Mowing foreclosed homes is easy work. There is no homeowner to complain about the job and it gives you a chance to make first contact with the new homeowner when they move in.

This is exactly what one of our friends from the Gopher Lawn Care Business Forum is doing. In fact, it's how he got his start in lawn care. He wrote "I'm just starting my lawn care service and to be honest I'm a little nervous. I got here by accident. After being a real estate agent for several years my business was killed with the housing crunch, so I went back to driving truck. I drove a truck for most of my life. I did network marketing too and then was offered a business cleaning up bank owned homes. What I found was after you clean them up you get the lawn service. Normally they want two cuts a month for $100.00. I now have 17 homes, so I decided to expand it to regular homes."

What advice do you have for lawn care business owners who are looking to get into the business of cleaning up bank owned homes? How can they get their start and are there any hints you learned or downsides to it?

"I got into cleaning up bank owned homes by accident. I had a friend doing it and he needed some help just cleaning the house (I had a cleaning company 10 years ago). After I started cleaning some of his homes, I spoke to a real estate agent I knew that was selling REO's (bank owned homes). She referred me to another company. When I called them, they asked if I could give them a bid to do everything, clean out the trash, clean the house and do an initial lawn cut.

My real estate friend gave me some average bid numbers for my area and included in all bids is lawn service. The companies that handle most properties are called preservation companies and most are nation wide. I haven't been getting too many bids lately I went from 2 to 3 a week to 1 every two weeks. The area where I live has a ton of people doing this kind of service. The preservation companies have web pages to fill out vendor applications.

Another good way is to look at the signs on bank owned homes and call the agent that has a lot of these properties and ask them if they are getting good service, they deal directly with the bank sometimes. There is competition in bidding. Bid too low and you don't make enough. Bid to high and you don't get the job. The worst thing about all this is I figure it will phase out over the next year but I could be wrong. This is why I'm trying to reach out to more regular homes."

Great advice if you are looking to expand into providing service on bank owned properties. Remember, once you get one property in a newer area, make sure you reach out to the neighbors with your door hangers and flyers to help expand your route. Maybe use a lawn sign in the front of the property as well. This one property could become your beachhead in your marketing attack to help you expand out farther and farther.

Marketing lessons we can learn from a realtor turned lawn care business owner.

If there is one group of local business people I find that are constantly hammering me with direct mail marketing material, it's realtors. They really seem to have their act together when it comes to promoting their name and face out to the local community. So lucky me and lucky us when a new Gopher Lawn Care Business Forum member joined up to say hi to everyone. He shared with us his story on how he got started with his lawn care business and some marketing secrets he learned as a realtor.

He wrote "hello everyone, I just wanted to say hi and introduce myself. I'm just starting my lawn care service and to be honest I am a little nervous. I got here by accident. After being a real estate agent for several years my business was killed with the housing crunch. I learned a lot about marketing in real estate, but the most important thing is you can't beat a referral from a happy customer!!! When my wife and I started out in real estate we had no budget, so we made up a flyer's that we dropped off on door steps. We picked a good geographic area with 200 homes. We made the flyer with cool and interesting facts. We also included a recipe of the month and what the housing market was doing.

People loved it, but you have to know that you must hit a person 6 to 9 times to be noticed and you have to stand out. Fridge magnets are a great marketing tool. One of the best fridge magnets I have used is a fridge calender for clients, so your name is always on their mind. Constant contact is key, and follow up with this line:

OH BY THE WAY…
I'm never too busy for your referrals!!
Talk to you soon"

Great advice from someone who knows what works.

Co-market with a garden center to gain more lawn care business.

When you are looking to gain new landscaping or lawn care customers, consider reaching out to your local garden centers. Purchase your supplies from them and see if you can get a business card display at their registers. Then ask the staff who sell lawn and garden supplies to refer your lawn care business for any install projects.

One of the Gopher Forum members in the past had hooked up with a garden center and gave the store employees 10% cash of each job total, when they referred a customer to him to do a job with material that was purchased at the garden center.

Because of this, he had consistent business referrals all year round. He was always doing so much better than any other landscaping business around him. So the lesson he told me from that experience was cash referrals can make a huge difference in your bottom line.

I asked him, how did you work out payments to the employees who referred you business?

"Every week I simply stopped in at the garden center, if I wasn't already there buying supplies and I would just thank the person and pay them cash on the spot."

Another thing you can consider doing is some cross marketing with the Garden Center. You could hand out flyers with your ad on one side and the garden center ad on the other. You could do the same with the door hangers. Then you could either split the printing costs or have them pay the printing costs and you go door to door to distribute them.

You could even host classes on the weekends at the garden center on how to install certain landscape projects. If the customer finds doing the job themselves is too overwhelming, they can always call you to help them do or finish the job properly.

Team up with a real estate agent to promote your lawn care business.

Real estate agents are the first people to really make contact with new home owners in your area. The agent has already built up a bond with the new home owner and is in a great position to refer your services to them. Why not team up with one or many real estate agents in your area. Help them create a welcome to the neighborhood kit and give yourself a head start jump on your competitors.

One of our Gopher Forum members wrote us on how he got involved with a real estate agent to cross market his lawn care business to new home owners. He said "while I was working yesterday, a real estate agent stopped to talk to me. He has built a great referral program and a service package that he gives home buyers when they buy a house. He told me he wanted to put me on his "preferred" service providers list that goes in these packages.

Right away he gave me a coffee cup with his all his information on it and a Thanksgiving card and small candle for my wife. The candle had all of his information on it as well. What a great idea!

He told me he would help me make a flyer like the one he gave me which was very professional and nice. Also hew said he could help me grow my business, based off of referrals. I only talked to him for about 10 min because it was getting dark and I had to load up and leave.

On the front of the card there was a picture of a family around a Thanksgiving table that says "Happy Thanksgiving, thanks for making me a part of your life." On the inside is a recipe for pumpkin pie dip. It says his name and real estate office then "A referral is sending someone you care about to someone you trust. Thank you for trusting me." I think its a great idea with the recipe and all. It also came in a bag with the candle.

I thought the card with the recipe inside and the candle with info was pretty cool. I'm going to do something like this with my Christmas cards. He seemed to be doing good with it."

I really like the idea. He positions himself to be the go to person in the community as he creates this network of contractors in the area with his referral group. This not only helps him build good will with the new home owner but he also builds awareness of his services through his contractor contacts. Both sides benefit.

"He called me last night and gave me a customer to contact for some work. I'm going to there house tomorrow for a bid. I was surprised. I have talked to a lot of agents and usually don't hear back from them. He said to let him know when I want to meet with him so he can help me make up some literature. He can probably give me some great ideas on a referral program since hes been so successful with his."

Does he want a referral fee for this? Or how does this work?

"No fee, he just expects the same in return. I run into people about twice an month that are selling their houses so I will refer him. He had a very good presentation for his service package and referral program. A notebook full of colorful, laminated pages that he has spent some time on. Not just something he threw together."

That is fantastic. You should contact other real estate agents to do this with and get a hold of more contractors as well to work together on welcome packages.

"I went out and gave the new home owner a bid and got a $650 job this weekend!"

This is a great example of how networking with others in your area can really help you reach out to more potential customers with minimal expense on your part. As we all know, keeping your expenses to a minimum is very important, especially when you are just starting out.

Marketing your lawn care business only with business cards?

Here in this economic slump we see daily posts on the Gopher Lawn Care Business Forum about the difficulties lawn care business owners are having as they try to find new lawn care customers. One of our members had an opposing marketing view that is held by many. He is finding a lot of success now. Let's see how he is doing it.

He wrote "well these last few weeks I have been completely covered up with work. I have picked up several new yard accounts, plus 6 tree removal jobs at about $700 each (average). I have picked up 3 brush clearing jobs. One at $600, one at $1,900, and another at $4,250."

That is great news! Can you give us your advice on how you stay busy? What should other lawn care business owners be doing or thinking about in order to get back on track? Especially if they recently got started?

He replied "well, most of my work comes from repeat business and referrals. Most of my new business comes from online classified ad sites. I have never spent any money on advertising, except business cards. I have a theory that once you start paying for advertising, you will need to keep paying to keep the work flow coming, so I've tried to avoid it from day one.

I would suggest just putting yourself out there, and never turn down an opportunity to talk about work with someone. I have started up conversations with MANY people about what I do, and the next thing I knew I was giving a bid to them, or someone they knew.

So I guess, talk, talk, talk, and put yourself out there. Let everyone know what you are doing, and don't be afraid to ask someone if they need something done."

What a fascinating insight! Now I would think not spending any money on advertising except for lawn care business cards would put him at a disadvantage, but it seems the opposite has happened. It is quite possible to make up for the lack of customers he would have to deal with by not paying for advertising, he has compensated for by being personable and working on his social networking skills. So I think this is a great lesson for us all. If you want to succeed and sell more, you need to talk more. Talk to anyone and everyone and let them know you can help solve their problems with your services.

Marketing your lawn care business outward from the center.

When the economy takes a down turn, there usually are many new opportunities for entrepreneurs to get started with their own business. A lot of times people will think about starting their own business but if they have a full time job, the job will most likely take priority over starting a business. But if you get laid off, you then can jump on the opportunity to finally start the business you wanted. Here is a great question and a great example of an entrepreneur taking advantage of his resources and his knowledge to get his new business off the ground. In the Gopher Lawn Care Business Forum the member wrote "hi I am totally new to all of this. I mowed lawns while I was younger and throughout high school in my neighborhood and can do just about anything there is. I was just recently laid off at an excavating business because people are not wanting to build new houses or buildings right now.

Right now as I am just starting it is frustrating trying to get new accounts. Beyond lawn care, I also am doing snow removal. I am not too good at this whole internet deal but I managed to start up my own website as well. I am trying to make a flyer right now with my plan to make around 1,000 flyers and just start going door to door. I do not know any other way to just get my name out there.

What are the best ways to go out there and get customers? Are there any suggestions out there to make my company look better than the others? I just want my company to stand out more than others so we look like we have been in business and so people would come to me more than other lawn care businesses Thanks to everyone for the help!"

I think first off you should jump on promoting services you can offer right now, that can make you money now. If your new business doesn't start making money quickly, you may lose interest in it or others around you may push you to consider other alternatives. There is nothing like making a profit to show the nay sayers they were wrong and you are right.

So how do you do this? Get on the Gopher Forum and download some of the free winter snow plowing templates. I have a bunch of them for snow plowing and holiday light decorations. Edit the flyers as you need to and start handing them out to family members and friends. Get business cards made up and hand them out to everyone you know. In fact, give them a couple each. Tell them you are just getting started and you would appreciate any work you can get.

Market to your inner social core first. That would be friends and family. Have them become spokespeople for your business and have them help get the word out about your business too by telling their friends, co-workers and community organization members. Hang up flyers where ever you can, such as in local stores. Go door to door and hand out flyers that promote your winter services. The more people you meet, the better your chances are of landing a new customer.

You had also asked about standing out more than others.

First off you have to remember, people will prefer hiring someone they know over someone they don't. So if someone knows you, that is the best way to stand out. Second off, get yourself set up with a uniform. Figure out a color scheme you want to wear and get a shirt and khaki pants along with a hat to match. This will help you look professional and presentable. Then get signs for your truck and trailer. If you need a business logo, remember I have hundreds of free lawn care business logo templates you can download and use from the Gopher Forum. Answer your phone and always be friendly and approachable, this should help you win many people over.

Lastly if you have time, you should consider doing something that is both a good deed for your community and a publicity stunt of sorts to attract media attention. Since you will be offering snow plowing, why not consider starting a volunteer group that clears walkways and driveways of snow for elder members of your community. Contact the local paper and tell them you are looking to form this group and you will be heading it. Have interested volunteers contact you at your business number or contact you through your website and ask for those senors in need of free service to contact you as well. Possibly offer it on a scale of the neediest first. This could be a great way to get your picture in the local paper and get the word out about your new snow plowing service. It will also build up goodwill within your community and free publicity. One simple article could really get your business launched.

So try these ideas out and let us know how they all work.

Lawn Care Flyers - should you include prices?

Should you include prices on your lawn care flyer or should you say free estimates and present the lawn care estimate in person? Let's look into question.

We were having a discussion on effective marketing practices at the Gopher Lawn Care Business Forum and there were quite a few viewpoints shared on this topic.

I asked the lawn care business owners if they included prices on their flyers and this is what they had to say.

One business owner said "when I go door to door to distribute my flyers, I put the price for that specific house on it so if they don't like the price they don't call. It also has every thing they will get for the money ie. monthly, weekly, or bi-weekly mowing. I also include a coupon for landscaping."

What is your view as to why you put a price on your lawn care marketing flyer?

"Well I put my price on them because my area seems to have a lot of tire kickers. They want the cheapest lawn care guy so they'll call around and go with the lawn care business who gives them the number they are looking for. Also you get those one time lawn cuts calling because their family is coming and the grass is 3ft. tall.

I don't have time for games. In my lawn care flyer I show you this is what you get, this is your price as I view the front and my knowledge of the average back yard in the area. The mowing price can go up if the back has a lot of work or I have to use my 36″ mower. I've gotten a good or better than average response with my lawn care flyers.

I put out 1,000 lawn care flyers and ended up with 3 mowing clients. The problem is, when it's time to distribute the lawn care flyers it's also time to cut the lawns. That marketing window of opportunity will depend on where you live. Either early or late winter. I would say as soon as the grass gets some green to it people see it's a lot taller than they thought."

Another owner said "I think meeting the lawn care customer face to face helps & I'd also like to think my clients aren't necessarily hiring me on price alone. I'm not the most expensive lawn guy in town… but I certainly am not striving to be the cheapest, so a little salesmanship may come into play."

I guess on one side, you can say I put my prices on the flyer and the customer can take it or leave it and if they call they are basically saying I know your price and I am willing to pay that.

On the other side is the customer that calls for an estimate. You walk the property with them and give them a price and if they flinch or say no, you can play with the figures, within reason to try and land that job. That is where being there in person and the salesmanship factor is important. If you don't get the job then you wasted your time going over there and giving the estimate.

The thing I wonder is, ultimately can you command a higher fee by making the presentation in person, because isn't that what an estimate is? A sales presentation?

If you can command a higher price, does it make it worth your while over other estimates you may have went on but didn't get?

"It's worth it to me! You are not going to get every lawn care estimate.

1. You have to remember that you can't take rejection personally when you are in sales.
2. If you're getting every single job you estimate YOU ARE LOWBALLING and you are leaving a lot of money on the table.

To make a "sale" the customer has to buy the SALESPERSON, the PRODUCT, & the PRICE. If you're not there in PERSON presenting the full value of the PRODUCT then they are only buying the PRICE. You didn't "make the sale", You are "ON SALE"!

Take the time to meet your lawn care customers, yeah you'll waste time on some but you'll be more profitable & both you & the client will be happier doing business together. You may meet some people & see a personality problem right off the bat… Then you can decline to estimate or work for them (I've done that once) or price it high enough it's worthwhile even if they are a pain in the ass!"

The last opinion on this discussion was"I've always leaned on the side of giving prices only during final negotiation. It's hard to convey your work ethic which justifies your price without a face-to-face meeting.

Though there are lots of tire kickers, I've found equal numbers of people will wait until their lawn needs attention right away. Once they call, they are ready to make a deal. If you can demonstrate the skill set needed to make their lawns look great, you can often command higher prices at these final meetings.

On-the-other-hand, if your price is on your lawn care flyer you've already set a ceiling which is difficult to raise."

I do hope this insight helps you determine better if you want to include prices on your lawn care marketing material or not.

Does your lawn care business marketing have a call to action?

There are many ways to promote your lawn care business through various forms of marketing. When you are creating your marketing, do you include a call to action? If you don't, you might be wasting your money. I had a chance to talk with a Gopher Lawn Care Business Forum member who had at one point worked as an advertising manager and had quite a bit to say on the topic.

He wrote "despite what a lot of the "never discount" people say, you really need one if you are going to advertise. I spent years as an advertising manager for a local media group (which included the largest newspaper in my area). When you find yourself debating on a "as low as $xx" statement, a discount, or something free. Free always gets the best response, but is also the most costly. Also free with a large stipulation (annual agreement) is not as good. I know this is redundant, but I learned a little about direct mail and it's always been about three things.

1. The right prospects. You can't sell lawn service to residents living in apartments or poor neighborhoods (maybe).

2. The right time. You have to hit them when it's relevant. The start of the season is a big time, but so is through the season, as unreliable lawn care business owners start screwing up.

3. The right offer. You have to give a call to action. Most folks will have already picked up a paper, phone book, or some other means if it was urgent.

If you don't do all three, it's just branding. Which is great for large companies that are looking for name brand recognition, but not folks searching for a measurable ROI (return on investment)."

These are some great lawn care business marketing tips to keep in mind the next time you are creating your marketing material.

A lawn care business sales secret.

When you are getting your lawn care business started and you don't have many personal contacts, the situation can be rough. Let's take a look at what our friend and fellow Gopher Lawn Care Business Forum member did to go from getting no return calls to many.

He wrote "so my flyers & business cards have been sent out all over, a lot of my cards need to be restocked in stores because they are almost all gone. Yet I have gotten no calls.

I only have a few days left, I can only do so much. I'm mass producing flyers again & plan to send them out to the other areas of my city.

I myself have walked door to door handing out 7000 flyers & I'm losing it! I don't wanna be out for weeks distributing these flyers so I'm gonna just start a.s.a.p. without stopping until they are all out! Can someone tell me what the hell I'm doing wrong."

You are doing a fantastic job. What you are doing with your flyers and business cards is good, however, you will find more success selling people to people. Selling to those you know or those that know you.

Have you considered picking up the phone and try to sell to people who are existing customers or people you know?

Then what you can do next is work the neighbors of your customers. Tell them you are servicing Mr. Jones' lawn and you would like to service their's too.

He wrote back "alright, I decided to reach out to my snow removal customers. They have all received my flyer, but they didn't know it was me offering lawn care service since I changed my business name. Once I talked to them and they knew it was me they insisted on hiring me.

I told them, the starting price for lawn service is $X.00, but because your you, & you helped me out during winter, it will only be $X.00 – a discount.

You can't beat that price, but hey, they were also my winter customers so they already know me.

I now have tons of appointments next week...

I guess I learned something. Call people & SELL yourself!"

Remember this when you find yourself having a hard time getting your initial customer base. Call people you know.

Advertise your lawn care business on garbage cans.

A lot of areas won't let you put out a yard sign on your property to promote your lawn care business, but what if you put a sign on your garbage cans to promote your lawn care business? This could be a great way to build out your routes around current customers. Maybe keep the sign simple and to the point "LAWN CARE - 555-2192."

You could also possibly put signs on your customers' trash cans and give them something like a free annual aeration or something like that in return.

I never see ads on garbage cans and because of that, they might stand out.

Maybe you could allow each customer to use a can of yours that said yard waste on the cover and was used for yard waste? You could then take the can back when their lawn care contract ends.

The great thing about this is garbage cans will be on the street usually twice a week and people driving to work in the morning and coming home in the evening will see them.

To do this really cheaply you could create a stencil out of card board that you can use with a can of spray paint. Anything you can do to get the word out more about your lawn care business is a good thing, so keep thinking!

How to find lawn care clients when business is slow.

The lawn care and landscaping industry is a seasonal business. Each season brings about a change in the environment which effects what services you can or can't offer. In the winter months, customers will also be looking to spend their money on holiday gifts. So with all this going on, how can you make sales with all of this working against you?

Here are 4 simple steps you can follow to drum up new work and sales.

1. Go through your customer list and contact inactive customers. See if they need any end of the year yard or home handyman services to prep up their house for the holidays.

2. Create a lawn care package special. For example, offer your current clients a discount if they resign up for lawn care service next year and pay you in advance. Maybe offer them a 5% or 10% prepay discount.

3. Repackage your services or products to make them more attractive during the holiday season. What if you sold a gift package that included a toy snow plow truck with a gift card attached that said Free Snow Removal for the winter. Or you could do something similar for lawn care service for the following year.

4. Wouldn't that make a great gift for someone's relative? What if it weren't just a toy snow plow truck but a collectible keep sake Christmas ornament? It would be a great visualization of what service they would be receiving throughout the winter months.

5. Experiment with new services. If you haven't offered holiday light decoration services why not consider that?

If you do decide to offer such gift cards, make sure you promote it. Send out flyers to your current customer base and hand them out in your community. Wouldn't such a present make a great gift? Maybe use the headline 'Show someone special you really care with free snow removal all winter long.'

Keep these ideas in mind when you are trying to drum up business in the slow season.

Marketing your lawn care business in an area with 14% unemployment.

A lot of areas around the country are dealing with high unemployment rates. When you are just getting your lawn care business started, you may find this adds to the difficulty of getting off the ground. A new business owner got on the Gopher Lawn Care Business Forum and shared with us his frustrations. He wondered what might he do to stand out in a highly competitive environment.

"Hello all" he wrote "I live in Oregon and we currently have the 2nd highest unemployment rate in the nation (just a tad behind Michigan). In my county our unemployment rate is almost 14%. This is my first year looking to start my business part time. I've landed a few lawn care jobs, but all by one have come from family or friends of family. All of my marketing has fallen flat.

Over 1,000 door hangers and only 1 call. Advertising in the paper, not a call yet. Updating my online classifieds ad every 2 days, no calls. I'm starting to feel like my market is just too over saturated.

I have a normal 8-5 job and see at least 1 or 2 lawn care business owners on the road every day. Sometimes up to 5 or 6 (this is only a 7 mile drive). What's happening in your areas? I'm considering direct mail or search engine advertising as my next advertising campaign, but am starting to feel like I am throwing my money away."

You can expand your marketing message or you can also experiment with the services you offer. When you talk to your family and friends are they telling you what their view is on paying for lawn care at the moment? Are they cutting their own lawns more often?

Have you thought about offering other services that many homeowners can't or won't do? Are there things your friends and family are saying they need help with?

He responded "most of them are cutting the lawn themselves. Even some who have over 6 figure incomes. Others have always had the same guys doing it. I don't want to lean on them to fire their current person just to hire me. That just doesn't feel right. A lot of the work I've been doing is non-mowing jobs. Like clearing a weed thatch, spraying herbicide, dropping some bark, replacing dead trees etc. I'm not sure what else I could offer, I'm sure you have some ideas?"

I think just making it known you are available is important. For instance, what if their sewer line backs up? Could they call you to snake out a line? You can rent snakes for $50 for half a day and charge a couple hundred to do the service. Most home owners aren't going to do that themselves. There are plenty of other services they won't do either.

This isn't about leaning on your friends or family to fire their current person. Everything is in a constant state of flux. New people move in. Old people move out. Your long time handy-man moves on to somewhere else. These things go on day in and day out. All you want to do is be that friendly face they know they can call to solve their problem.

Maybe a fridge magnet would keep you around until they were ready to call you.

I would keep letting them know you can help with all sorts of things. Changing a hard to reach light bulb. Cleaning out gutters. Fixing a roof leaf. Trimming back a tree. Reseting a mailbox. Replacing a sidewalk?

I bet if you asked around, each person has a to do list for their home, they never get to.

Maybe put together a lawn care business flyer asking potential customers what's on their to do list? It might get people thinking about their long to do list. Everyone has one and no one ever gets it done."

He responded "Thanks, this has given me more to think about. While I had wanted to try and focus on my core business (mowing and maintenance) I might need to branch out a little to try and find clients."

What your core business is today may not be your core tomorrow. Experiment and see what works best for you in your area.

Lawn of the month marketing campaign.

Here is a lawn care marketing idea that you could use to attract new business with little investment.

What if you created a lawn of the month contest. Create a yard sign that says lawn of the month and each month pick a different lawn you service to become the lawn of the month. Stick the yard sign in the lawn and show off the property on your website. In your website, show the reader why you decided to chose this property as the Lawn of the Month.

Create a lawn of the month flyer. This flyer could say something like "We at Joe's Landscaping are pleased to announce the lawn of the month for Oct. 08 is Jim's lawn located at 123 Main St. When you have a moment, please drive by their property to view it. I hope this yard inspires you to create ideas on how your yard could look. Please give us a call and we will stop by to provide you with a free landscaping analysis. Our analysis will show you what we could do to improve your yard's aesthetics. Call us at 555-8372.

Hand these flyers out to homes in the area of the lawn of the month home.

You could even present the homeowner with a trophy or a certificate that you printed out on your printer. Take a picture of you handing the homeowner the prize. This is a great way to build your customer retention levels. If a customer feels appreciated, they are less likely to choose another awn care service provider.

Send a press release to the local paper with the photo and a little write up about your award and why you chose this property. You could also do this in conjunction with a local home owner's association.

Recession marketing ideas for your lawn care business.

A new lawn care business owner had a very unique marketing idea that had a political edge and wrote us about it. "Hello! Just joined here and was looking to get opinions on a couple of truck magnets I designed for my boyfriend's lawn care business. I pretty much handle his marketing/advertising and recently noticed some local business putting out specials/adverts using the down economy angle. My boyfriend is currently/interchangeably displaying one on the back of his tailgate above his website address and opposite his regular business magnet.

The concern is that he's a little worried the magnets may seem a little political/controversial. Personally, I think they will draw attention to the business/website because everyone can relate in this current economic climate and the text doesn't force an opinion per se (but I could be wrong).

I am aiming for potential conservative, liberal and indifferent customers appreciating the magnets in a (hopefully) neutral and humorous way. I want to increase the website traffic while being more noticed and seen as distinctly different amongst the current competition around town. He just started the business in May of last year after a layoff and is 30 accounts strong right now just by himself. We've baby stepped everything, pretty much in a methodical/grassroots/DIY level from the beginning."

I can totally understand his point but you know, to me that's what marketing is all about. It's all about being different. If it can be controversial, even better. You want people to be talking about your marketing and if it isn't different, if it doesn't stand out, then you aren't going to get attention.

One of the things that I have been amazed with is that it takes soooo much energy to get a business started and running, and you have to really be different from the average person to even attempt it. But why do the same people who are the adventurers, the crazy ones, those with enough energy to start a business then decide they have to keep things tame in their marketing? Why do they not want to stand out? What makes people so afraid to stand out? To be different? To gain attention? Especially when that attention can get you more work?

Take for instance, Richard Branson, owner of the Virgin empire, such as Virgin airways. Recently he was promoting his airline dressed in drag, in a cheerleaders uniform with a blond wig. Guess what. He got media attention and here we are talking about it.

If you don't do something different, you can only at best expect the same results everyone else gets.

So for all this, I applaud you for being creative!

"Thanks for your comments! Regarding the political marketing truck magnet angle, my boyfriend was uncomfortable with it on his truck and removed it about a week ago. I kept the picture of it on the website, however, but with the lead-in tag line above it that says:

DON'T COUNT ON BIG GOVERNMENT TO PROVIDE YOU WITH ECONOMIC STIMULUS,

SAVE MORE GREEN SO YOU CAN SPEND MORE GREEN WITH JOE'S MOWING!

I think I will create a new magnet along those lines. Next time around, perhaps with dollars signs swirling about and/or superimposed in the background.

As far as the bail-out special we created and 10% off on prepays 3 or more months, more people have utilized the 10% off prepay promotion so far. Although we just recently created the bail-out special. I think by next month's billing cycle we will know if our monthly customers will be taking advantage of the 5% discount. We don't advertise/push promotions yet to existing customers by emailing or snail-mailing them notifications. Although they are always encouraged to check the website for updated promotions and specials when they sign up and we note the Refer-A-Friend savings prominently on their invoices.

Right now we feel it's the customer's responsibility to check our website on their own. Our plan, sometime this year, is to send periodic postcards/emails to existing customers (quarterly or so) to remind them of updated/new specials and offer them (suggestive upsell) tips. We could do monthly tip, etc. emailing, but it would be annoying and spam-like in my opinion.

We currently have about 6-7 solid prepaid accounts. It was a bit hard to do prepays in the beginning due to it not generating regular cash flow. However, the couple of ones that we had in the beginning did help to fund some start-up equipment purchases. Once we established over 20 accounts (and we hit 35 officially this week!), prepays have been a nice chunk of change when the payments comes due. A prepayment on a new account today just helped us purchase a new backpack blower!

I am definitely all about interrupting the mind with different types of marketing a la Mr. Branson. I am actually thinking about investing in a fluorescent green bear mascot suit in time and holding a very prominent advertising sign for the business (with the website, of course) and dancing a VERY animated jig on the side of major roads just to see what kind of response it gets.

When my boyfriend goes out on an estimate call and meets with customers he often tells me about the positive feedback he gets regarding our door hangers and website, most especially. We offer a lot on our promotions on our specials page, all things we will honor in a heartbeat, but not as many people take advantage as you'd think (so we're not losing our butts per se). The general consensus seems to be people do NOTICE our marketing attempts/specials and do respond positively without being prompted. My speculation is that they feel that they seem to be getting 'more' with our lawn service versus with the general competition and consider us a more value-added option, if only 'psychologically'.

Again, thank you so much for your comments! I love this website! I'll keep posting on successes and misses."

Why not prompt the customers though?

For instance, why not come up with a special say Spring flowers planted in your yard for $X9.95, but hurry and contact us by XX/XX/XX date. We need to get your order into our supplier to be able to offer you that discounted price.

Then a week before the date, send one last reminder email maybe upping the ante. Offer some additional option if they call you by that date.

The world goes by pretty fast and I like getting updates on sales when it's something I am interested in. I think others do as well. Don't you?

"I like and can see your point about using more direct and active 'prompting' with the way you presented that Spring flower special example. I just may try something like that and perhaps show a sample before and after picture pre/post-flowers, tree trimming or mulching via email or postcard to add a nice visual. Thanks for opening me up to the possibilities!

Delivering more than a customer will normally expect and providing a great first impression is more the guide for my 'speculation'. Be it on site, online, in advertising or on the phone, etc. it translates to more bang and service for the buck, which they definitely get in reality."

So keep all this in mind when you are experimenting with your lawn care business marketing. Don't rely on the customer to seek out what your specials are. It's up to you to tell them. This is all a part of selling.

Lawn flyer distribution tips.

When you distribute your lawn care flyers, how do you do it? Do you have any specific method you use? Have you found one way works better than another. Well here is a suggestion from one of our forum members that might help expand the way you think about this topic. He wrote "I just recently came up with a couple different forms I'm planning on using. These aren't my primary flyers however as I am experimenting with them. One is to stir up new business this year and the other is a pre-printed estimate sheet that's on a heavy weight pre-folded paper."

Very creative! How will you be distributing them?

"I was planning on targeting very large developments and just going door to door either leaving them on the mailboxes, or on the front door. The sheet that has the section for mulch is my "estimate sheet." That's the form I use when I receive a customer call to come to their property and give them a quote. One problem I am running into is after I give the quote, how would you suggest following up on it?"

That's a good question. Do you try to seal the deal on the spot when you give your estimate or how do you go about giving your estimates? Do you leave them in a mailbox? Is the customer present?

"Most of the time when I am giving estimates no one is home, they are usually working. By the customer's request I either leave the estimate in the door or in their mailbox. I think handing the customer my estimate face to face would be ALOT easier to close the deal and get a contract signed right then and there but its not a perfect world so what do I do for the customers that I am forced to leave the estimates for them to review???"

Another business owner suggested "it is always better to give your estimates while you are standing with the customer. It's more likely then, that they will give you the go-ahead. The exception to this is if it is a large job and you need to go home and run the figures and do some calculations. Even then you should present it to them in person after your figuring is done.

Another thing is after you present the quote, and they want to look it over, wait 3 days then call them and ask them what they thought of the estimate. If they have reservations, ask them what the issue is and see if it is something that you can be flexible on and maybe meet them in the middle somehow. Follow these simple rules and I promise you will land more bids!"

I agree. I think if you try experimenting with this, you are going to see a big difference. You can also judge the persons reaction to the price and if the price seems to be a sticking point, you can always ask them what you need to do to get their approval so you can start today. Maybe you could give them a certain % discount on the spot to get the job.

Being with the customer allows you to feel out the situation.

"In person is best. It is easy for folks to say no, or just flat out disregard you, when you are not there. Like someone else said, if you are present you can feel out the situation and perhaps make some changes to seal the deal. You may have to sell why you are worth this money when your competitor charges $10 a week less.

If you are having problems being able to meet in person, you may want to play on the angle of liking to make in person contact so they know who they are potentially dealing with and who will be coming on their property to mow while they are not home. When you make contact, find something you have in common with them, but don't get too overly personal with them if this is the first time you meet."

I hope these ideas help you land more lawn care accounts.

Lawn care business flyer door to door distribution advice.

For every lawn care business start up that exists today, there is a theory on how best to distribute lawn care flyers door to door. Everyone seems to have their own way to do it. Everyone thinks their way is the best way. Some put flyers in the door without knocking. Some put flyers in the mailbox. Some knock on the doors first. But which one of these will give you the best return on your efforts and money? Let's see what some of the members of the Gopher Lawn Care Business Forum had to say about this topic.

One member said "I remember exactly how it was when I was first starting up my lawn care business. I would spend-spend-spend and then wonder why I wasn't getting slammed with new customers! Flyers ARE great, but what's better is FACE TO FACE time with a customer and a professional image! I would recommend creating a 'script' of sorts and practice in front of a mirror so that your delivery is smooth and not forced. Get your opening lines down for when you first greet a "P.C." (potential customer) and most importantly BE YOURSELF.

After sending out 1,000's of lawn care flyers myself, I decided to invest in a 'uniform' shirt. It was just a pocket t-shirt, but it had my logo and I also got some hats. I would typically wear khaki or green work shorts and work boots too. And when the weather is cooler, khaki or green work pants. Blue jeans (and certainly not "cut-offs") were not part of my uniform. I just think it made me look 'unprofessional.'

Once I started actually knocking on the doors and TALKING to people, as I would gain their confidence and hopefully their business, I would then hand them a flyer, a fridge magnet and then…CLOSE THE DEAL. 'Would you like me to get started on this right away? I could begin by…..' You have to ASK for the order! Once you have them to this point, you know your time, your money, your effort, was all spent much more wisely than throwing darts blindfolded at balloons."

Another business owner added "Here is the best thing to do from my experience.

Collect flyers from other lawn care companies one year before you start & months before the start date of your first year. Look at the pros & cons, & get to work on creating your own lawn care flyer!

Distributing lawn care business flyers can get very expensive and it costs me valuable time. I also have to rely on many people, & when they decide to work making flyers, is when I'm out of time & have to rush.

I had an extra 1,000 lawn care flyers created Tuesday night. I took the day off to think & relax… Wednesday, I went & handed out 1,000 flyers by myself, & tomorrow is my last day before May. I still have to bust my *** to make this work. It never ends, not until your getting paid.

My thoughts;

You will never be done advertising even after you've been door-to-door to every possible house in several cities. I started off with 500 flyers, nothing happened, 12,000 flyers later I'm still preparing to mass print more. I might put together a team of 6 to hand them out for me at $10/hr, if I save on supplies I can spend on workers at least this one time.

You have to advertise when other companies do, & keep up with them. Most of them do the same homes 3 times! So your mission is to do so as well. Others may also use direct marketing so they don't have to bust their *** handing out flyers, but the cost to do this is ridiculous.

When to hand out flyers.

1st time: Before lawn service is needed, this reminds customers it's almost time, they usually toss it in the trash.
I got 4 calls per 100 flyers.

2nd time: Customers are taking the time to see what you offer compared to other services, it's still too early for them to give a damn. They will consider it when the time comes. In the garbage again!
This time I got 7 calls per 100 flyers.

3rd time: It's late, but the grass is looking good. Customers might have thrown out your competitions flyers & now have only you as their savior & last minute option. At this point lawn service is serious & needed.
I got 20 calls.

4th time: Yet to be fully discovered by me, but I believe if you can do it, you should!"

Keep all these thoughts in mind when you go out there marketing your lawn care business. Sometimes all you need to do is change one little element in your marketing strategy to really find success.

Positive press is good for your lawn care business.

Positive press can have a tremendous influence on how the public perceives you and your business. When people in your community hold you in high regard, they will want to hire you or purchase products from you. They will also pay a premium to do business with you because of the high level of goodwill you have within your community.

How can you get positive press?

I have two stories for you. The first involves an elderly woman who lived alone and lost her home to a fire. In the local paper, on the front page was this sad story of how a local senior citizen lost her home to a fire. It included a picture with smoke billowing from the old house. When the reporter asked her how she felt about all she had been through, the woman said what she was most upset about was that she lost her wedding ring in the fire.

The next day, a local jeweler was reading the article and he jumped on the opportunity to help out. He contacted the paper and said he wanted to help make things right by offering this woman a new ring he would create and present her for free. WOW did this make the news and this jeweler looked like a superstar. With a front page article on him the next week presenting the woman with a new wedding ring, he could not have paid to get such great attention.

Another great story was told to us on the Gopher Lawn Care Business Forum by a member. In his post he said "When my father was a lawn care business owner he saw a news show on another lawn care company company who screwed a 90 year old lady out of a job she paid them to do. They took a 50% deposit & never landscaped her house. It was on all over the news. My father thought this was awful & that it spoke badly of all landscapers in the eyes of the public. He contacted the old lady, met with her & arranged to do the job for her for free, he was just going to pay for all the materials out of his pocket & install them. He didn't intend on getting media attention but the old lady called the news station back & told them how this nice man was going to complete the job for her for free. They ran another piece on the local evening news, with that several nurseries contacted the news station & offered to supply the materials for free. The press did another story & interviewed my father while he was on the job & took a few shots of it after completion. My father got calls from people impressed with his generosity & wanting him to work for them for YEARS!"

So think about this the next time you see something that you feel isn't right and you can make a difference.

Make a section on your lawn care business website and include all the press you have received and make it a mission to do good deeds. Collect future news on you and share it with visitors who come to your site. Use it in your other marketing material as well.

Easter promotion ideas for your lawn care business.

As business owners, we can take each holiday and use it to promote good will within our community and promote our lawn care business. All we need to do is add a touch of creativity and from where there was nothing, a new promotional idea can sprout. Such an idea can help you reach out and promote your lawn care business to your target market.

One of the things you could do is host a local Easter Egg Hunt in your neighborhood. You could have it at your store front, or on your property or at a local park.

Get a bunch of plastic Easter Eggs and fill them with treats. Then hide them in different locations and let the kids run out and find them. They can be hidden in the open or out of site. Give each child that partakes, a bag or a basket to hold their eggs.

Maybe have special gift baskets for the first X amount of children that attend.

You could also dress up as the Easter Bunny and have pictures taken of you in a costume with the child sitting on your lap. Post these pictures on your website and have them available for download in their full size, by the child's family. This would be a great way to show off your community involvement and attract people to your site. On your site you could offer a holiday special package if the customer signed up by a specific date.

To promote this, you could send out messages through your online social network site. Or you could put the information on a flyer / door hanger. Have one side promote your event and maybe the other promote your lawn care business with your holiday special package available for a limited time. Make a post on an internet classified ad site about this. Depending on the size of the event, put an advertisement in your local paper. Create lawn signs to promote the event. Send out emails to your current customers. Send out postcards. Send out a press release before and after the event to your local paper with pictures of it.

This would be a great way to create a fun event that will draw in your potential customers and give you a chance to really stand out from your competitors.

Can you imagine if you do this for a bunch of years how it could really grow and kids will come back to you years later to tell you how much fun they had, thanks to you.

Try this out and let me know how it goes.

Fall leaf clean up marketing idea with inflatable Halloween decorations.

Halloween is a great time to put out yard decorations. There area many new items on the market to add some seasonal flair to your property. Some of them are inflatable and are lit from within for decoration at night.

Something you could do to promote your fall leaf clean up service is to use one of these inflatable Halloween decorations on your property and using a stencil, spray the message "Fall Clean Up 555-3029." It could be a great way to attract the attention of those walking by or driving by your home at night. You could also do this if you have a commercial location for your lawn care business.

You could even take this idea one step further and put up an inflatable Halloween display at the homes of your family or friends in town too to help promote your services further. Can you imagine how much attention you could get if you placed this at a busy intersection?

While you are at it, have you considered renting out such Halloween outdoor decorations to lawn care customers and providing seasonal home decoration as a service? It could be another way to make money in your slow season.

If you are out in your area raking up leaves and want to promote the service further to neighbors in the area, why not try this. Get some pumpkin leaf bags and on the blank side on the back, use a stencil to spray in your lawn care business phone number and maybe the words leaf cleanup. Place the bag where it will be easily seen by others passing by. Use one of these bags per job. That will really make it stand out and attract attention.

- Step 1. Get a bunch of orange pumpkin style leaf bags.
- Step 2. Create a stencil with leaf cleanup and your phone number.
- Step 3. Spray it on the bag with black paint and you got a great way to advertise.
- Step 4. Use one of these bags per job when you are bagging leafs to get the word out about your business.

Pumpkin & lawn care business card marketing.

I am always keeping my eye out for new and creative marketing ideas that can be applied to the lawn care business and I saw one that I thought was great.

Realtors who want to make money know they need to keep their name out, especially when people are looking to sell their homes. They also want to gain referrals of friends or family members through their marketing base. So the other day, there was this Realtor driving around with her SUV with the rear section of her truck full of these small pumpkins. She wasn't just stopping at every home on the street but instead stopping at the homes that were well kept and looked like they were worth something. Then she would get out of her vehicle and walk up to the stairs and place a pumpkin on their door step and leave.

I thought this was a fantastic idea. You could do this too. Why not get a bunch of pumpkins and tie some business cards to them. You could go out around town and distribute these pumpkins the way this Realtor was doing it or you could distribute them to the neighbors of your current customers using the clover leaf technique. This could really help you stand out and add more customers to your current route. The more customers you have closer together, the more profits you will make due to the fact you will be traveling less in between customers.

Maybe on the back side of the business card you could also offer a fall leaf clean up special! Play with this idea and you might find something that will work great for you.

Snow plow marketing idea.

Coming up with new and innovative ways to stand out with your marketing can be really tough to do. So if something works for others, why not experiment with the idea on your own. This marketing idea is sure to make you a favorite amongst your customers and neighbors. To promote your snow plowing services why not try this.

One of our forum members wrote us and said "Here is an example of some decals/stickers I made for my snow plow clients. I wanted to give out buckets of ice melt to my snow plow customers but wanted my name and company info on them. You can get any sized bucket you'd like and slap a sticker on the side that includes your logo. Above your logo you could have it say complimentary ice melt provided by. And on the bottom have it say, please call for refills. I also made "Please keep covered" and "Use Gloves" stickers for the lids.

The great thing about this is you can re-use the buckets every year. You can fill the buckets with salt, ice melt, etc."

This is just fantastic. There are many things you could do with this. You could buy a bulk amount of buckets and get these stickers printed up, then fill each one. Stop by the homes in your area and drop them off on the front stairs possibly along with a door hanger explaining who you are and that you left this free gift. If the customer would need winter snow plowing services, they could contact you and also don't forget to promote your lawn care services as well, for the spring. The cover of the bucket or the side could have a sticker that says something to the effect when it snows contact Joe's snow removal.

You could also include a coupon to help give the homeowner an additional incentive to call you within a certain time frame.

Now if you wanted to give these to only your paying customers as a thank you for signing up, you could go with a larger bucket but if you wanted to use them as a marketing tool and distribute them more widely, you could go with a smaller size.

"The salt buckets worked extremely well!"

Thanks for keeping us posted on how using them worked out!

In the field & operations.

Who would you hire to cut your lawn?

When you are showing up to meet a new potential customer, how would you rate the first impression you make?

One of our forum members asked this great question. "What do you guys drive when you give bids. I am not a huge company so a lot of the time I take my personal car.

Do you think that people want to see a nice company truck pull up? Gas prices are high and my cars get better mileage than my trucks.

How are you guys dressed when you go. Work clothes?"

One member wrote "I get lawn maintenance jobs because they see my nice work truck. It doesn't have to be new, it just has to look like you use it for work.

Customers will actually tell me, "some guy came here with a Toyota Camry…" to give me a bid and that really seems to turn them off.

They like the work trucks."

Another shared "I feel the same way. I go on bids with my work truck, I'll even go with the trailer and equipment attached, but I keep it clean and nice. My truck is not new by any means, but it's very nice and very clean, same goes for the equipment. As far as dress, I always keep a clean pull over golf type collared shirt in the truck to throw on when meeting a customer for whatever reason, appearance I feel is very important. Remember the customer's first impression is always very important, you don't want to come off looking like a slob."

A third business owner added "I always take the truck and trailer. I think customers like to see that you have all the equipment, etc. As far as clothes go, I usually wear work clothes unless I am dirty from working."

If you have been reading my blog or the Gopher Lawn Care Business forum for a while you know I like to keep expenses to the bare minimum. So even if your truck is a rust bucket, which is ok by me, make sure you have some type of signs on it to show that you are legitimate. No potential customer is going to want to hand over money to you if they think you are a fly by night operation. They want to see that you are legit.

How many lawn care accounts can a 1 man crew maintain.

A Gopher Lawn Care Business forum member was looking for insight into how many lawn care accounts he could possibly service as a one man show. He asked "for the single person crew, how many lawn care contracts are needed to maintain a healthy income. I was thinking 40. My brother-in-law does good on 25 but he also does a lot of brush hauling and debris as well. I am only doing lawn cutting and trimming with some hedge cutting and gutter cleaning. My average is $25 per lawn cut. I currently only 10 lawns per week.

One response was "I wouldn't be so worried about the amount of contracts but rather the amount of income, and what you can accomplish within a week by yourself, without working too many hours.

I have 25 lawn care accounts for a monthly gross income of $4,700, and the only help I receive is on Fridays. My buddy helps me all day for $100/week. I could actually accomplish all the work myself, but the help on Friday is very nice. Most of my accounts are larger complexes, with only a handful of residential customers.

When I first started my lawn care business, I went to every property management company and introduced myself, and started with a few on some smaller projects and worked my way up within the year to larger complexes. I would say 90% of my customers are projects where a previous lawn care service provider was terminated and I was hired in their place.

So if there's any advice I could give out, it would be to make sure you do the little things like pull the weeds and rake the flower beds, oh yeah and keep that grass green, cause these things are what people want and expect, and matter most."

How close to your working capacity do you feel you are at? Are you maxed out at 100% or do you feel you still could take on more accounts?

"I would say with the help I get on Fridays, I'm at 80% capacity. This includes taking care of a few properties close to my house on Saturdays. I work very fast and efficient and hard. I don't skimp on any detail of the work that needs to be done, which is why I've been fairly successful.

It's funny, I've pulled up to a house to work and see another lawn care guy at a house next door already mowing, with yards of equal size, I'm done and pulling away and this guy is still edging, with blowing still left. I think some guys assume the longer they are on site, the better job their doing?? I can also see this same guy doesn't pull the weeds in the landscaping?? Some people out there I guess are just out to make a quick buck, but I'm in it for a lifetime. Even when I can't do the work anymore, I'll hire someone."

What do you think contributes to your ability to work faster?

"I would basically say speed, I don't dilly-dally around like I see some of these other lawn care guys doing. I get in, get the work done, and get out. I suppose I get into a routine and get a consistent work pattern. I simply go from 1 step to the next without stopping. I guess you could say I'm great at time management.

By not dilly dallying it will save you time but it's your routine that makes the money. In my area, if you edge the lawn before you mow then you'll have compressed moist dirt into the concrete. That takes a lot of time to clean up. Also if you line trim the grass first, you have to trim with both sides of the trimmer head but if you cut first then your only using one side. These are some time saving ideas that have allowed me to out worked up to 3 others at once."

How much money can a solo lawn care business owner make?

A lot of times a new lawn care business owner will be working solo and wondering what kind of income can they potentially make? How many lawns can the average solo lawn care business owner service? To get some insight I asked some lawn care business owners to share some of what they have found as a solo lawn care business operators.

One lawn care business owner said "I work by myself. I can get most of my average $25 per cut lawns done in 20-25 minutes. Once I have done it a few times & have the lawn under control & "trained" the way I cut it, meaning the grass isn't too long, the trimming never gets out of hand & the edging has been done before so I don't have to dig out the edges of a driveway that have been covered over 2 seasons ago!

I have a few I can mow in about 17 minutes. Here is my lawn care routine. When I arrive on scene I check the time, get out of the truck, mow, weed eat, edge & blow off. Trailer closed ready to roll, back in the truck. I hustle like heck though. I kinda get in a mode like a machine & keep going all day until my mowing list is done. I should say though, I've gotten very used to using a line trimmer to do edging. It's kind of an art form to do it right but it saves lots of time, the machine is in your hand & running already!

I can't really say what profit I'm shooting for per lawn, I've always kinda tracked it by time. When I'm out mowing I shoot to make $35-40 per hour. This is including travel time & my lawn care routes are not as tight as I want them to be. As I go down my lawn care mowing list, I check em off & mark what I made on that lawn today. Keep in mind with my monthly lawn care accounts in the summer, if I get $85 per month & I have to cut it 4 times that month I count it as $21.25 for that cut. Some months I have 5 cuts, so I rely on the per cut accounts to keep that figure up in the summer time. Last summer I shot for & usually hit about $225 gross billed per day. The most I ever did in a day by myself & it happened to be the hottest day of the season (103 deg., 98% humidity, & 106 deg. heat index) was 15 lawns with 4 of them overgrown for a gross of $650.

As far as cost per lawn I don't know, If I could do a month with x# of lawns (the same lawns) every week I could figure it out, but it varies a lot I'm sure. The property lot sizes here are 80ft x 125ft = 10,000 sf subtract the average house, garage/driveway and you get about 7,500 sf or lawn. I do have some vacant lots I mow for a customer once a month so they don't get fined by the township.

With the mower I use I had to remove my mulch kit to do it (which I charged $250 for the 3 lots to knock em down) after that I mow once per month with deck all the way up at 5″. I sold it as "field mowing" & let the customer know it wouldn't be perfect, I'd make 1 pass (flying) & keep the township off their back but that I wasn't going to abuse my machine like that (it's not really that bad) for less than $50 / lot. So I go once a month & make $150 in about 45 minutes.

I have heard of a few guys that are $30-35+ a lawn in the area I think the majority are priced around me or lower. I understand If you push quality & demand more money there will be some takers & eventually higher overall profits. But that's easier to do once your busy as heck. Raise your prices & don't take any new work unless at a better rate then slowly drop your less profitable accounts as you replace them or get them to raise up too. I average $35 or better per an hour with travel time because I can do a 10,000 sf lawn by myself mowed, trimmed, edged & blown off in 20 minutes."

What kind of mower are you using to do this?

"I have a 52″ 23 hp commercial zero turn. Zero turn is the only way to go! Pushing a mower is too tough to do. I won't even take on a lawn that I can't get my mower in (fenced etc.) Not worth my time & uses too much energy on 1 lawn."

How do you suggest coming up with a pricing strategy?

Another business owner said "my pricing strategy was based off of other companies; I called them to get quotes for my lawn (~2500 sq ft) and came up with a strategy that brought me in below all their prices. I've had a couple friends bring in quotes for their properties as well, just to get a comparison, and I've always come in near or at the bottom.

I guess based on your market you'd have to adjust…I find with all the trimming and blowing added in, my pricing strategy works out to about $35/hour billed (which is what I charge for most other labor).

I mow all by hand with a push mower…I used to take about an hour or so to do a 2,500 sq ft lawn, but I've gotten faster after a couple years of doing it.

I still have the same pricing, but it probably takes me about half an hour or so to do 2,500 sq ft with blowing and trimming/edging."

A third business owner wrote "I won't cut anyone's lawn for less than $30.00 a visit and I don't give any price breaks for annual customers unless they pre-pay for service at least a month in advance. I think you could be making a bit more money if you could differentiate yourself from your competition. I am a new company and have no problem doing this.

Here's an example:

I did a spring cleanup, 16 yards of mulch, trimmed 60' of hedges, planted 18 annuals, 5 perennials, and charged $1,485.00. My profit for this job was around $950.00. How did I do it? I played the game and talked the talk with the customer, made them feel like they had found the very best landscaper in town. Don't get me wrong the job looked great when I was finished but the perception of the customer was far beyond the one man crew (me) that did the job."

Another member said "I also started with a 22" 6hp push mower, but my blade was razor/chef knife SHARP! With the blades sharpened I could go a little faster. Manually mowing was one of the hardest thing I've ever done and I was doing like 5 houses (only 1 day though). At the end of the day, I was done and totally drained. But then I bought a 32" commercial walk behind, I love it!

In my area the competition is real tough! I've seen online classified ads that said "mowing starting as low as $10/cut" I don't know how they do it either. My cuts go around $30 or $60-

$130 a month. So I say that we are around the competitive prices in my area."

I hope this insight helps you compare your business and see how you are doing.

Profit markup lesson from an outdoor power equipment dealer.

I know you are probably sitting there scratching your head and saying, I don't get it. Why are we talking about profit markups from a mower dealer. Well the first reason why is because it was very informative and secondly because we need to keep our ears open to all types of industries so we can learn from them and apply what we learn to our businesses. This discussion started off on the topic of dealing with customers. From that it morphed into a profit markup lesson that I just had to pass on to you.

We initially were talking about using free online classified sites as a way to attract lawn care customers and I had said "I think this is something that many lawn care business owners on the forum have found. These free classified sites are full of tire kicking customers and cheap customers. However it is a good way to get your feet wet and get the gears of your business spinning. Once you get yourself going, you should constantly be on the look out for newer, better customers that you can either add to your current customer base or replace an older low profit customer with.

I think you may find that 10% of your clients take up 90% of your time. Ultimately, it's my view, these are the customers that need to be replaced. You should enjoy your business and if you are finding yourself getting ground down by unhappy people that are also your customers, look to replacing them with others who aren't so nit-picky and are more profitable."

Another member joined in and said "I think I have to concur with you. I personally feel like there are certain customers that "the competition" can have. Years ago, when I was just a kid, a young guy from our community decided to open an outdoor power equipment shop. This person happened to be from a kind of "uppity" family. I recall his dad standing in our mower shop and telling my dad that we were charging too much on a particular item. I knew for a fact that for the $70-80 item he was talking about, my dad had marked up no more than 10% from actual cost. Just for the record, there is no way to operate on a 10% overall mark up. The minimum to "survive" in this industry is about 25% due to a number of reasons.

Anyway, when this guy started his shop he made it clear that he intended to put my dad out of business in less than a year. My dad said, first of all, there is enough work for both of us, and second, he will attract others like him who will be looking for a "cheap deal." We started sending those type customers to him. He shortly told my dad that he just can not afford to stay in business. Meanwhile, my dad has never had to advertise and has never suffered from a lack of work, even now, over 10 years later......

So I guess the moral of the story is, you kinda get what you pay for. You may be able to get some good customers on free internet classified sites but be aware there are many "bargain hunting", "tire kicking", "cheap" customers out there. As a business, always be looking to keep customers as happy as possible but don't cry if the cheap ones move along to your competitor..... There comes a time when a customer costs you more than they are worth. But still, you just want them to go away, not go away mad......"

Do you feel there is a national average on markups at power equipment dealerships? If so, what would the range be? And what reasons do you have to shoot for 25%.

I bet a lot of these reasons apply to a lawn care business as well.

"Actually I meant to say 20% but for the sake of the conversation lets go with 25% like I said. I find myself charging more like an average of 30-40% mark up. The quick answer is to help with lost labor costs and overhead expenses (electricity, tools, thousands of dollars in parts investment, etc.). I am a small shop and estimate a total tool investment, both special tools and non-specials tools, of about $500-750. This is one set of tools, mostly Craftsman or second hand tools.

I have come up with some generic figures and examples that I remember off the top of my head.

The reasons for a minimum of 25% mark up are multiple:

1) I purchase a product today for $2, stock it for 2 years and sell it for a 25% mark up at $2.67. Now I go to restock and find myself paying $2.35 for the same product. I have now made $0.32 on a 2 year investment. A $0.35 rise in product cost can easily take place every year, but again, this is for the sake of conversation. We need to look at the parts as interest bearing investments.

2) I have had to take the time to order the product, stock, enter in computer inventory, pull from shelves, and invoice for the sale. Let's say the average dealer in the US only charges $30 per hour labor rate (average is above $60). If this take even takes me only 3 minutes to complete (order, stock, enter in computer inventory, pull from shelves, and invoice for the sale) I am doing good. Now figure up the labor cost associated with this: $1.50. I have now lost $1.12.

Let's say the product costs me $60.00, shipping included. Now my profits are $20.00 minus my costs to order, stock, enter in computer inventory, pull from shelves, and invoice for the sale. Now my profits have fallen to $18.50. Unfortunately we can not mark up this much on every product but on some products we can do more. Every shop has at least one or more items that literally costs them money to sell.

3) 'Part' profits help defray $$$ lost in labor. The actual national "billable labor" average is currently believed to be 60% or lower. What this means is if I employ Joe as a mechanic and pay him for 8 hours per day, I will only be able to bill 60% of the 8 hours (36 minutes out of every 60 minutes) to my customers. If I pay Joe $10 per hour with no benefits, he has cost me $80 for the day. If I can charge 60% of his time to my customers today, I have had an "above average day" and should be able to charge $144 in labor. That makes me $66 for the day while Joe made $80 today. And I have all the headache of the shop and he goes home after 8 hours while I continue to slave away over paperwork.

So this is where that extra $18.50 for profit helps. If I charged only a 10% mark up on that product the figures would look like this:

Product cost: $60 + Mark up: $6.67 = $66.67 - costs: $1.50 = Profit: $5.17

Now I would have made $5.17 on a $60 investment. Not too bad if it comes in and I handed right over to the customer who installs the product. But if my shop installs it and it takes 30 minutes to install, I have probably lost money.

So you ask, where do the other 24 minutes of the hour go?

Consider this scenario:

Tom, the homeowner, brings in his riding mower. It has a flat tire and off the bead because it was sitting like that all winter, does not start, has a hydro tranny, needs a tune up, and checked over. Joe grabs the clip board, gathers Tom's info, the mower and Engine info. Tom tells Joe what he wants done with the mower and Joe notes this info on the work order. This takes 4 minutes. 20 minutes left. Joe gets ready to unload the mower. Since the tire is flat and off the bead it will have to be lifted or dragged off the truck or trailer. It has a hydro tranny so it does not roll when in neutral.

Now I have to help Joe unload and move it into the shop. 5 minutes later we have it unloaded and in the shop, read to work on it. 5 minutes x 2 = 10 minutes. Only 10 minutes left. During the next 5 minutes Joe takes the engine and mower info, looks up and picks the parts required for the tuneup and repair. 5 minutes left. Tire is fixed, mower is tuned up, and Joe starts the mower and takes it for a test drive. takes 1 minute. Joe returns to the shop and completes the invoice and calls Tom to tell him the mower is done.

Tom lives 2 miles away and is at the shop by the time Joe completes the invoice. Tom has arrived. 5 minutes have been used up. They load the mower, Tom looks the mower over and decides he likes the way the engine starts and is happy with the service. Tom and Joe go back to the shop and Tom pays Joe. Tom asks Joe a question about his old chain saw and string trimmer. They decide the saw and trimmer are not worth spending money on. They have taken 10 minutes to do all this. Now we have robbed 10 minutes from the next hour....... Oh and we have forgotten to figure in the 3 minutes it took me to order, stock, etc. the part......

How does this apply to a landscaper? I'll let a landscaper give us a scenario on an "average job", say a mow job, on that.

Remember all your overhead expense of running your truck/trailer, buying gas, cost of maintenance, drive time, unload/load time, time spent signing contract, obtaining payment for services, etc. You also have to figure in the original cost of your equipment, anticipated repairs needed (i.e. hitting something in the yard and needing to replace a bearing assembly and blade, etc.). I am sure there is some type of equation available to determine the estimated repair/maintenance cost of a machine.

I suppose if you expect that a mow job takes you 30 minutes you need to be able to charge around 1 hour labor. You have to figure all this in."

This is a fantastic insight into the operations of an outdoor power equipment dealership but it also applies to a lawn care business. As he said, you have to account for everything if you are looking to make a profit and be in business for the long haul.

The danger of large lawn care accounts.

It seems like every year I hear a similar story in different variations. A new business is just getting itself stabilized with a hand full of customers when a large account seems to be calling them from up high atop a mountain of promised money. The call becomes so enticing that the entrepreneur can not stop themselves from holding back.

Does the beginning of this story sound familiar?

This time the story revolves around a lawn care and fence installation business. The business had been started the previous year with just the owner running it with a helper from time to time. The owner also had a full time job to cover his expenses. All was going fine. The business was growing slowly until that fateful phone call came in. This large commercial property needed lawn care and a fence installed.

The job was going to be a big job but the owner was going to have to float the project for 60-90 days. That is how long it would take to get his first payment. Could the owner do it the caller asked. A big fat five figure project was just waiting for him if he said yes. So he gambled and said what the heck, I deserve this, this is my time to step up, and he said yes.

At the time he started this job, he had managed to save a few thousand dollars. He thought this would be enough to get him and a few helpers through the next 2 month or so. The next day, he quit his full time job and showed up to this commercial facility to start work.

The grass was tall and un-kept so it took more time than normal to cut it down. The fencing. The fencing was going to cost him big money that he didn't have. He would have to pay for this on his credit card. He would also have to buy a large commercial mower on his credit card. But there was no risks right? I mean he would most certainly make his money back on all this and them some. Right?

Within a handful of days from the time he took the call. He had quit his steady full time job. He had hired a few extra helpers. He had depleted his savings and gone into a 5 figure credit card debt.

After the first month he submitted his invoice and was elated. Never had he submitted such a big invoice to anyone in the past. He was finally a big lawn care business. He already had plans to upgrade his truck and trailer. He made it.

The second month rolled on and he started to get nervous, especially when he saw the for sale sign go up. He called and asked about that. Surely he was still going to get paid right? Oh sure they said, you will be paid. He was getting worried because he figured he had about 3 more weeks of living on his credit card before it was maxed out.

Now do you want to guess what happened?

The check never came. The commercial property was sold. He never got 1 penny. He lost it all. He had to quit working on his business and get another full time job. And he will never ever be able to start another business again. His wife has threatened him with divorce if he ever brings it up.

Listen to me when I say this. There is a non-stop supply of such stories. Prevent this from happening to you. Start small and scale up. Grow at your own comfortable pace.

5 simple steps to improve your lawn care business.

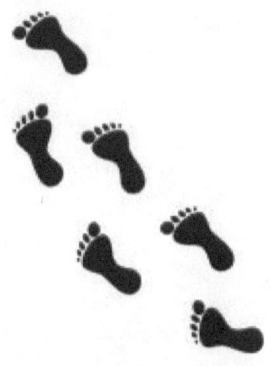

When you are trying to get your lawn care business to grow, think of these 5 simple steps you can easily follow.

One of our forum members wrote "I currently have a lawn mowing only operation, and it's worked out very well for me. My travel time is very low and the routes are tight, with a two man crew averaging about 25-28 lawns per day. This works great in my area, however if I tried this where I grew up in in another state, I wouldn't have a chance. It definitely depends on the market you're in, as well as what rules you set forth to the customer.

I've had absolutely no complaints this year, and most people are on credit card billing. I attribute this to "choosing my customers" rather than them choosing me.

My lawn care business is only mow and go and has been for two years now. I only use postcard advertising hand delivered door to door to gain my customers. We run 21″ commercial mowers, no trailers, two trimmers and 1 blower. Basically everything is paid for, and with 22 lawns or more per day, things are going well. My next step is getting out of the truck and starting another crew. I have learned a great deal from my first year doing this, mostly:

Keep it simple! I decided to narrow my business down and focus on the 5 main things that I needed to focus on and the rest would take care of itself. If you focus on the most important 20% of your business, you will succeed.

The 5 for me were extremely simple:

1) Find a cost effective way to distribute postcards. I always without fail generate a 1.2 - 1.8 % landed job rate from my cards. So basically it's a sure bet if 5,000 go out, I'll always get 60 customers or more. How do I distribute the postcards? I'm considering a direct mail route next year, but I do like the door to door as they at least have to hold it in their hand for 20 seconds on the way to the trash.

2) Do quality work! This sounds like a no brainer, but in fact my major competition now has a huge turn-over of customers from year to year. Although my business method involves somewhat of a revolving door scenario, retention is a key priority now for me. This DOES NOT mean I stray from my guidelines of service however. It's about a win-win situation between you and your customer.

3) Strive for automation. I've had almost 80% of new customers sign up online without ever talking to them. There's nothing better than coming home to 15 e-mails of people signing up for service with their credit card ready to go.

4) Answer phones and return emails promptly! While missing calls can possibly cost you a job, make sure your voice mail

directs them to #3, your website to sign up. Always leave them with YOU in mind. I currently do not have a phone person, although that's going to change very soon. However, with the proper voice mail greeting you can have people signing up anyway. (Provided you convince them with your website)

5) Maintain your equipment. Again, a no brainer, but honestly I was running low on things to make my biz successful while putting it together. Over the winter this came to mind for the #5 slot. There's nothing worse than trying to start a trimmer on lawn #15 of that day and it not starting with 8 more lawns to go.

I should also say that I pay my help extremely well and I only work with people I respect and admire. I am not doing this solely for income, but for personal satisfaction and achievement as well. Therefore, although I do watch P & L and numbers carefully, I would much rather create a successful work environment for everyone in which we all can grow. This has always paid off for me in the long run, as it's universal law and cannot fail."

Great advice we all should consider!

The benefits of lawn care business job tracking.

One of our Gopher Forum members shared with us his view on material usage tracking. I think his insights are very helpful and will lead you towards a proper path.

When Winter arrives, it's time to start the year end preparation for the next year supplies and materials. This can be helpful if done properly.

Do you track the materials you purchase throughout the season such as mulch or fertilizer? If not, you should, and here is why.

- In order for you to grow your business you must set realistic goals.
- If you're not tracking how much product you purchase, how are you to know how much or how little to buy for the next season?
- If you do know, your one step ahead and then you should set a goal and prepare for it. This means what you bought in product last season you should increase 20-30% each

year until you reach your customer base goal.

Knowing how much materials used on a job/customer will help you for the next season, making you more efficient and raising profit margins. Growing you business.

Setting goals gives you an incentive to attract more customers. Be realistic when setting these goals, some call it baby steps I call it setting a customer percentage increase or CPI for short.

Without tracking, how are you to know if your growing or not? Most that do not track will never make it in lawn care business. 80% will fail in the first 3 years of starting their lawn care business.

I track everything, fuel, cell phones, mulch, fertilizer, weed control, right down to the uniform pants we purchased. I can tell you how many 'Moon Shadows' we bought last year and these are our trade mark plant. The total was 46. I can tell you how much we spent on pavers and wall block on each job. This comes from job costing or known as tracking.

Why is this so important? Well let's say:

- First it saves you money when taking your books to the accountant, because if he/she has a shoe box full of receipts and has to go through them to sort it all out just to do your taxes, you just lost money because their going to charge you for the extra time it took them to figure out what is what.
- Second, it helps you to be profitable in knowing how much material you used and cost of it.
- It also helps you set your CPI for that service.

Even more important is that you will find extra money in the bank and think wow we are doing great. You may find yourself asking can I afford that new Z turn or that new mini skid-steer I was wanting this year? So off to the bank you go and the first thing the loan officer asks is I need 2 years of tax returns and a P & L.

Opps you didn't track or do proper basic bookkeeping and now your P & L looks like like a train wreck. So now you're back looking at them saying well this is what I came up with on the P & L. Here is the total amount of jobs we did and here is where we paid all of our bills and here's what we got in the account so I guess this is my profit. This might work but I personally don't care for a 'might.' I am more of a yes/no, right/wrong type of person, no gray area. I don't have room for it in running my lawn care business.

When you are presenting yourself to the bank as a lawn care business owner, you should at the very least appear to be professional and have proper basic accounting practices. This means just because they have known you at the bank for some time doesn't mean they know what kind of business person you are when it come to handling business finances. Saying it and doing it is two different things. You'll find most bankers are like Missouri, the "Show Me" state.

Bottom line is proper accounting practices and keeping up to date with them will make you more efficient and profitable for time spent. If you're spending 3-4-5 hours a day just doing paper work and trying to catch up on the accounting then you need to work on time management. Proper time management can be beneficial to everyone especially your family. Set a time schedule and stick to it. My schedule is 8am-6pm M-F and every other Sat 8am-noon. After that I don't work on business stuff.

If you lack the accounting skills to be proficient, check with your local Library for free computer classes in accounting. Ultimately you will thank yourself for getting onto of this.

What will make your lawn care business look professional and make you more money.

Have you ever asked a new lawn care customer what complaints they had with their previous lawn care service provider? I bet if you did, you would get an earful. I asked this question on the Gopher Lawn Care Business Forum and got some interesting responses I want to share with you. Here are some of the responses.

"Most of my client's biggest complaints about their previous company was on these topics:

- The guy did good work but was unreliable & went too long between cuts.
- I signed the contract with him for monthly billing & he started scalping the lawn so he didn't have to come nearly as often.
- I signed the contract with the guy & never saw him personally here again & none of his lawn care employees speak English!"

Now let's jump to a story that involves one of our newer forum members. He is 17 and he runs his own lawn care business. He writes: "How do you save to prepare and buy future lawn care mowing equipment? I want to buy new everything. Besides a landscaping trailer, which I already bought. I have everything but it's old and I want it to look professional. The reason I want new equipment is I'm trying to be as professional as possible. Many people don't think I'm serious since I'm only 17. But I am, so I'm trying to show it more."

This is a problem many new lawn care business owners run into. They think newer equipment will promote a more professional image which will lead to them finding more jobs and making more money. However I can tell you the Gopher Lawn Care Business Forum is full of posts from business owners who are no longer in business. Why? Because they focused on issues their lawn care customers couldn't care less about. Customers don't care how new or old your equipment is.

If you want to do something to promote your level of professionalism, spend $50 and buy a couple of embroidered polo shirts and get some khaki pants and a customized baseball cap to create a business uniform. Get a sign on your truck and trailer to show that you are legitimate. Lawn care customers hate the idea of handing over money to someone who looks like they are about to take off out of town, never to be seen again. People want to feel secure and sense some kind of stability. They want to know you will be around. They want to see you around town and know that you are involved in their community.

Look around your town. Most start up lawn care business owners don't wear any kind of uniform and have no brand image at all. You create brand image for cheap and you will be the lawn care business that stands out. Let me now jump to a post to show you a real life case of what I mean.

A lawn care business owner wrote "well in my area the lawn care businesses usually have business shirts and tan pants on. They have signs on their equipment. I knew this guy who ran a very successful tree company. The thing was, he was quite a goofy guy but he was smart when it came to marketing. Here is what he did.

Every single piece of equipment he ever bought he would always have it painted bright yellow. I mean everything was yellow! He had tons and tons of different trucks and tree hauling equipment. But his love for "everything yellow" did NOT stop there. He made the outfits all bright yellow. He ordered custom work boots that were yellow and had the company imprinted in the leather. Every single personal car he had was yellow. He was a pretty wealthy guy so he had a bunch of cars and crap always sitting in his driveway, including 2 big motor homes trailers, dump truck you know…everything.

The whole moral of the story is, every time I heard people talking about his business they always referred to it as "that business that has all the yellow stuff" and he was well known for just being the color yellow. You know it might not be the nicest looking color in the world but it got him SO much business.

I talked to him about 2 weeks ago and he now owns 3 big shops/warehouses/storage areas and has small cranes and a few bucket trucks. He has really grown!"

Look professional, act professional, create a brand and your business will grow. Only buy lawn care equipment as absolutely needed. Don't spend yourself off a cliff. Stay out of debt.

Don't try to compete with $15 bucks a cut, stand out and command a premium.

Are you finding yourself trying to compete with fly by night lawn care businesses that advertise they will cut a lawn for $15? Don't try to compete with them. Any customer who hires such a lawn care business will quickly find out how unreliable they are. You don't want these cheap customers anyway because they will be the ones most likely to complain. Instead why not follow the steps these other lawn care business owners have taken. Be personable. Meet with your new potential clients. Offer them an incentive to prepay for their lawn care and give them the best service you can.

One of our Gopher Forum members wrote "I've found because there is so much competition in my area that lawn care prices are held down a bit. Once you have a good lawn care customer base & you give them good service you can:

- Raise prices a bit more as you've had a chance to prove yourself to them.
- Go higher on new estimates as you don't really "need" every new customer.

Now I am, to the best of my knowledge, competitively priced for my area as far as my per cut prices. Some are higher & I think that is attributed to being well established as I stated above. But there are advertisements in the newspaper here and on internet classified sites for my area that promote $15 bucks a lawn mowing! Granted most of them are probably in it for extra beer money & are unreliable to their customers but my potential customers see those advertisements too & know if I bid $35 per lawn mowing they can get it for probably half that however lousy the service may be.

My annual/monthly clients are required to pay by the 1st of each month for the following months service. I'm afraid of cutting for a month billing them net 30 then cutting for another month & finding 2 months in that they don't pay so that's the only way I will bill for that type of customer."

Do you offer any incentives for your clients to sign an annual contract instead of staying per cut? How do you pull that off?

"Sure I offer incentives. It has helped me find better lawn care customers as well. I no longer will mow someone's lawn on a 'per cut' basis. I have found out that those type of customers are not the ones we should be looking for.

You always 'need' new lawn care customers. This is how you grow your business unless you are comfortable with keeping it a one man show. I personally don't want to stay in the labor end of the business forever.

I try not to run my business the way everyone else runs their's. Get a business plan and stick to it, that's what I did and it's proving to be successful so far. Also, the people that a '$15.00 a cut' advertisement attracts are NOT the customers you want. I had to learn that the hard way."

Another member shared "I think I am in the same boat as both of you. I am trying you find a good overall price to charge my lawn care customers. This is my first year really trying to push the lawn care. The lawns I work on are a lot bigger than what most people mention here. The houses all sit on 1/2 acre lots if not bigger. The houses average 2,200-2,400 sq ft, 2 car garages with long driveways. When I started calculating everything my game plan is to charge $35-$40 a cut, offering a 15% discount for the customers who sign a year contract and pay up front.

Now I thought I was reasonably priced until my clients start getting quotes for $20-$23 a cut. Luckily I have 6 yrs of sales & marketing behind me. By presenting my lawn care flyers that are professionally laid out and knocking on every door I hung a flyer on, I was able to sway every customer to spend the $15-20 extra. I personally couldn't believe it and neither could my girl friend who helped me distribute the flyers. The only problem with this strategy is that I don't cover much ground. Out of 100 houses, I talked to maybe 1 to 3 people who were receptive and willing to sign a lawn care contract.

The way you present yourself is everything. You're not selling a product, you are selling a service. I am always more expensive. I don't try to be. I just don't want to work enough to just pay my bills and break even. I hope this helps."

Is striping lawns a normal service?

We have all seen some lawns that really pop. As you drive by you can't help yourself but to look at them. Dark lush green lawns with stripes can really get a lot of attention but is that a normal service to offer? That's the question a lawn care business owner wondered when he asked "Is striping lawns a normal service?"

Another business owner said "I think it depends on where you are. In the south grasses such as Bermuda and Zoysia do not stripe well at all because of their growth habits "runner grasses." Although you can "burn" stripes in runner grasses. You just cut the exact same pattern every time you cut the lawn and eventually it shows up. But it's not good for the grass to do this. In the south, Fescue will stripe well but that's about it. If you are in an area where you can grow Rye grass, Fescue, Kentucky Blue etc "clump grasses," you can make striping look nice.

It is also one the most efficient ways in terms of time to mow. You make a pass turn 180* and make a pass next to it. But you have to make sure you keep the mower straight. No one wants banana shaped stripes.

IMHO I think it comes down to the type of grass you are cutting and if the owner wants it.

When you see stripes in grass you are seeing where the mower past. If the mower was going away from you it shows up as a light stripe. if the mower was coming towards you it makes a dark stripe.

Striping a lawn is a great touch especially for customers in higher priced neighborhoods when you can charge for the extra effort needed to make stripes look professional.

Specific grasses and well irrigated lawns make for better stripes."

How to lower your lawn care business fuel costs.

Gas prices can play a huge factor in the profitability of a lawn care business. If you are looking for ways to lower your fuel costs consider these ideas a Gopher Lawn Care Business forum member shared with us. Lawn care operators and professional gardeners get a little nervous as the gas prices creep up because it means their bottom line is creeping down.

No one is immune to the rising cost of energy but our industry is affected to a greater extent because we provide on-site service which entails driving trucks around. How can the average LCO reclaim lost profit due to dramatically increasing prices at the pump? What can you do to reduce the energy costs in your business?

1. **Raise prices** - The obvious answer is to increase your prices to recover profit lost to the increased cost of fuel. If you are not already considering the cost of fuel in your pricing, you should be. Having said that if you are a new company trying to break ground or if for some other reason you feel you cannot raise your

prices for some of your customers you may have to absorb the extra costs. If you do this, it should be part of a calculated business plan and not done haphazardly.

2. **Efficient Routing** - 'Windshield time' is always a killer of healthy profits but now more than ever is it important to ensure your job routes are efficient. Take a hard look at all of your routes to make sure that there is as little backtracking as possible. Have a look at a city map to avoid taking 'scenic routes' to your jobs. Can you juggle your routes so that you are avoiding high congestion areas at peak periods? Can you leave earlier in the morning to avoid rush hour traffic? Make sure your staff understand the importance of always taking the most sensible route. Consider using route analysis software to help with the task of routing.

3. **Focused Marketing** - Along the same lines as #2 try to build tighter routes where the properties are close together. A great way to achieve this is through focused marketing. Pick some neighborhoods that you are interested in growing into and hammer them with your marketing. Not just once but again and again. Be consistent with your message and this will build confidence in your company. If you have a property in the neighborhood see if you can get permission to put a lawn sign somewhere in the yard for a limited time. Eventually you will build super-efficient routes that require very little fuel.

4. **Driving Habits** - Studies show that driving at 55 mph is about 20% more efficient that driving 70 mph. Avoid rapid and/or jerky acceleration and use cruise control whenever possible. Don't use the air conditioner unless it's really necessary. Shop around for the best gas prices and take advantage of gas station loyalty programs that can save you money. Maintain your vehicles so as to improve gas mileage – this means regular tune-ups. As well, check tire pressure and alignment which can also affect mileage.

Don't drag a truck full of equipment (and perhaps even a trailer) around when you do your quotes – you're flushing money down the drain. Of course, there are times when you'll need to do quotes during the work day and you must use the truck, but try to avoid it. Consider getting a more fuel efficient car or even a motorcycle/scooter to do your quotes. If you thoroughly analyze your driving habits you may surprise yourself at where you can cut a few corners that can make a difference to your bottom line.

5. **Equipment Tips** - Tune-up your equipment. Smooth running equipment will not use as much fuel so keep your engines under a tight maintenance schedule. Consider using 4-cycle engines where it is practical, they burn less fuel (and are more environmentally sound too).

6. **Offer Great Customer Service!** - We are not the only ones effected by the higher costs of energy. Our customers drive too and they have to heat and light their homes. If you are making your customer feel important then you will not be on the top of the list of things to cut from their budget.

What's more profitable for a lawn care business, small or large yards?

This is such a great question and I am glad it was brought up on the Gopher Lawn Care Business Forum. There are up sides and down sides to going for small lawns or big lawns. For instance, if you service a lot of smaller accounts, no one customer will be monopolizing your time and if they cancel, it won't be a big shock to your business. However you will need to travel in between these jobs which will increase your wind shield time or drive time. As we have learned, you aren't making money when you are driving so you want to minimize the amount of time spent driving between lawn care customers.

Having a larger property to maintain can be beneficial because you will be providing lawn care on a larger area without having to drive around too much. Something to watch out for especially when you are bidding on larger properties is that new lawn care business owners have a tendency to underbid jobs. They just see $ $$$ signs and aren't taking into consideration how much it will actually cost them to service such a yard. This can lead to breaking even on large jobs or even losing money on them if you aren't careful. Let's learn more on this topic by talking to a forum member about how he prices lawn care for his business.

He wrote "prices vary depending on the market. No matter what, I suggest that you set a minimum charge for lawn care. My minimum charge is $35 with prices going up from there. This is for mowing, trimming, edging, and blowing off the grass clippings. However, I was talking to a guy from my area last week who said that he couldn't get more than $25 a mow. He even mows some lawns for as low as $15. What I'm saying is you must find out what your competition is charging, and what the market supports. Also, you must make money on each account. If you are not you must be charging more. Once you get going, figure out what your cost per yard is, and then set a minimum PROFITABLE price based on that assessment."

How do you estimate lawn service? Do you charge per acre or how do you charge?

"I do not charge by the acre. You should have an hourly rate for which you want your company (not yourself to earn). Mine is $45 per man hour. For example, If you have a large property that takes two guys one hour to mow you should be charging at least $90. It is ok to let this rate vary down a little bit, but not a lot. Like I said, my minimum charge is $35 which would be for a smaller, regular size yard in a residential neighborhood. I have one property that is about 5 acres(approx). It takes 2 guys about 3.5 hours to mow, trim, edge, and blow off. I charge them $250 per mowing.

Also, if you are doing fall cleanups. Make sure you are getting at least $45 per man hour on those."

What kind of equipment are you using on the larger properties and how do you estimate fall leaf cleanups?

"This large property is owned by a demanding customer who has extra high expectations. When I say it is 5 acres, this is 5 acres of well manicured fescue that the customer wants bagged. I actually only use a Walker Mower with a 48″ cut for most of the mowing. He has a area up around the house that he likes to be push mowed. This is done with a 21″ Toro. I run Stihl FS 100 RX 4 mix trimmers, and edger. He has a driveway that is approximately 200 yards long that is flanked by pine trees. Consequently, when trimming around the pine trees, the driveway becomes littered with pine cones. A large backpack blower is required to clear them in a timely manner. This is one of the accounts I inherited from my previous employer. When I was there we usually had 3 guys on it with 2 mowers. This knocked the time down to 2-2.5 hours. Usually closer to 2.5 hours.

I think fall cleanups are tough to bid. I usually try to help my regular customers out, and just charge them a leaf removal charge, depending on how much longer it takes us to mow it. I break down my per man hour charge into minutes. For instance $45 per man hour equals .75 cents a minute. If it takes two guys 10 minutes longer than it does to mow I would charge them $15 dollars extra. $1.50 per min x 10 minutes.

For non customers, who only receive one cleanup at the end of the season…a good rule of thumb is to charge twice the amount that you would charge to mow. However if the property has a high amount of leaves and complications such as beds that are tough to get to, or water features you should charge more."

What has been you experience on servicing high end properties and large properties. Would you prefer most of your lawns to be large like this and high end?

Or would you prefer your ideal lawns to be smaller and not so high end?

"I would prefer for all of my accounts to be high end. It helps company morale a lot if you are taking care of high end accounts. I have found that employees take a greater sense of pride in their work when servicing high end accounts. As far as the size goes, both large and small have their positives. The thing I like about large, high-end properties I just mentioned is that you are there for an extensive amount of time and always producing. The truck stays put, and you are getting output for the whole time. You can make the same amount of money mowing 5 or 6 smaller yards in the same amount of time, but your rig has to move from account to account. Therefore, I think the larger accounts are more cost effective. The downside to the larger accounts is that it tends to tire you and your employees faster, rather than getting a break from yard to yard."

Consider the pros and cons of servicing each sized lawn as you create your marketing campaign to target them.

What keeps your lawn care business small?

One of our forum members created a post to show off part of his fleet of lawn care business trucks. In the post I had a great opportunity to learn a little about what stops most small lawn care businesses from ever getting themselves up to that size. I hope some of these questions and answers can really help you push forwards farther.

With all these trucks, I would think you would be in a great position to have insight into why do you feel the majority of lawn care business owners never get to the size you are at now?

What keeps most of them small?

"Everyone has different reasons, but here are a few that come to mind.

1. They spend too much money on equipment, trucks, etc., before their business can support the costs. If you notice, all of my trucks are older but paid for. A nice new truck looks pretty and all, but I can do the same thing and only spend 1/10th of the cost.

2. Greed is a big killer. You must pay your helpers a decent wage to keep them. My lawn guys average $20+ an hour. I don't have the employee turn over that most do. My workers are paid a percentage of the job, so the more work they get, the more they make. This allows me to grow without worries of help being there.

3. Many lawn care business owners never dedicate themselves. They do the lawn work on the side as a supplement to their income and have another job too. With the security of their day job, many won't strive for growth."

Do you have any suggestions on how a lawn care business owner should structure their employee incentives?

"I give my foreman 20% of the job. The crew gets 15%. As an example, say you have a 3 man crew handling a yard that is being charged $35 per cut.

Would the foreman get ($35 x 20%) = $7
and each crew member get ($35 x 15%) = $5.25 each."

Contracts.

Should you go with a signed or verbal lawn care agreement?

There are a lot of new lawn care business owners just getting started and because they are new, they don't know where they can get away with using a verbal agreement when providing lawn care services or when they need to use a signed agreement. I want to use these recent discussion as an example to help you expand your business knowledge base.

A forum member wrote us and said "Here is my situation. I posted an ad on an internet classified site to perform lawn care for any realtor who has vacant homes that need lawn care. I was contacted by one wanting mowing, seeding, plugging, fertilizing and pine straw put out. This job was for two homes, both on the same street. I came up with a price for labor and got prices for material. I was then contacted and told I could go ahead with job.

The problem is I had no address to send the bill to and had not met anyone in person. I called back and asked for an address for which I could send an invoice to and guy said the work was for someone else and he would get back to me with an address. I have not heard from him as of yet. I am looking at spending $400.00 out of my pocket for materials to do this work. I think there should be a meeting and signing of a contract to ensure I am covered in getting paid for this work. Without any meeting or something signed if whoever decides not to pay, I have no recourse in recouping my expenses. I need to know from all of you if I am right and should not do any work until there is something signed to cover me and the lawn care customer so everyone gets what they paid for. All suggestions are welcomed."

A member responded "You are correct. I think you have plenty of reason to be concerned. I would not perform any work until you have laid eyes on the "lawn care customer" and, especially in this strange case, until you have a signed contract in hand. I think I would make sure the contract included specifically who is responsible for payment. Then I would make sure that the person signing the contract also prints his name (I would probably have a spot for him to "print" and another spot for him to "sign" rather than just having him sign and print his name below the signature.).

I think I would start out with drawing up the contract and then calling him to ask for a place to meet him or whoever is authorizing the work. Make it clear to him during your telephone conversation that no materials will be ordered and no work will be done until a contract is signed. Maybe even ask for some money upfront to purchase materials. This would help ensure they are willing to go through with the deal. I suspect someone is trying to pull a fast one on you. I would not lose a lot of sleep over the deal until you have met the customer and have a signed contract in hand."

Another member said "We have had past problems with realtors and owners who are actively selling/managing foreclosure properties. We only do prepayments with signed agreements for these types of customers now. We either meet with them for signing or mail them an agreement. They can provide guaranteed full payment or a good faith deposit in cash, check or money order or via PayPal. Once payment and agreement is received/cleared then the work will start. And so it goes with ongoing service.

With renters, we asked that they provide their driver's license # on an agreement in the event of defaulted payments."

Yet another lawn care business owner shared his insight by saying "Be careful here. Like other have said above, meet the client & get a contract signed. I have had 2 or 3 instances where a new client called, requested an estimate, I called them back & they approved the estimate by phone & gave a billing address. I did the work & got stiffed. Prepaid cell phones & BS billing addresses. I can't track anything at all, it sucks!"

These are great responses from people who are in the know. Don't be so desperate to get your business started and do this kind of work only to find out when it's completed that you can't find the person to pay you.

Annual lawn care contracts, the benefits and how to sell them.

Having your lawn care customers on annual contracts can be very beneficial especially during the winter months. If you are not so good at budgeting out your money and tend to spend what you have, then maybe having lawn care customers pay you an equal amount each month would be the way to go. The customer can benefit from this as well because they will be paying the same price every month and they can more easily fit it into their budget.

I asked lawn care business owners, what is the best way to present the annual lawn care contract concept to your customers?

One owner said "People are hesitant to sign up & pay $70-100 per month to you when they just met you & when the next few months the grass doesn't grow much.

I seem to have better luck during the summer with simply saying verbally: I also offer monthly billing, I know Mrs. Smith that $30 a week is a lot to pay for lawn care & this time of year that can mean $120 -$150 a month! So here's what I do, I'll do it for $100/

month year round. It's more budget-able for you & I can better budget my business knowing exactly what's coming in. Basically, I agree to make less during the Summer & Fall & you agree to help me feed the wife & kids in the winter time. Either way it's up to you ma'am. Which way would you prefer?

I did pretty well, No I didn't get every one. But I'd say more than half to choose the contract option!

The property lots here in my area are 80'x125' and if they are on a corner they're a little bigger. Last Summer, provided it's a normal house (normal amount of landscaping, fences, ditches to line trim around) I would quote $25/cut or $85/mo year round. I didn't specify much as far as frequency other than to say during growing season I'd be there weekly & out of season It's usually about twice a month. On a corner lot it was usually $30/cut or $100/mo.

A couple months ago as things slowed down with the per cut customers I really learned the value of those annual accounts & I need to stack on more annual accounts over the summer to be in better shape next winter. So I found a way to get the pricing more competitive & lean the cards so I would get more annual accounts than per cut (in theory anyway we'll see). Part of my new proposal form looks like this:

This proposal is for: the property at the address above. Normal services include mowing, line trim, edging, blow off all concrete walkways/driveways.

In this proposal the monthly fees are based on 34 services (visits) per calendar year as follows:

Month = # of visits to be made under this agreement:

- Jan.= 1

- Feb.= 1
- Mar.= 2
- *Apr.= 2
- May= 3
- June= 4
- July= 4
- Aug.= 5
- Sept.= 5
- Oct.= 3
- Nov.=2
- Dec.=2

Billing options: *Per cut (weekly In summer months) $ * * wk or Monthly billing with annual agreement $ * * per month.

So for example the same lawn I had been quoting $25/cut or $85 /mo. before I would now do this.

If I want $25/ cut: *$25 x 34 services/yr = $850 divided by 12 months is $70.83. Rounded up I quote $25/cut to $71/month.

My prices are more competitive & I still make $25/cut when all is said & done.

If they need an extra cut in there it's just that… extra!"

Now that is a very interesting way to sell the concept of the annual lawn care contract to new lawn care customers. Consider this when you are out there signing up lawn care customers as well. You might find the monthly price you quote on an annual contract, a little easier for the home owner to accept. You still get paid the same amount in the long run but the monthly prices are cheaper for the customer.

The pros and cons of using lawn care contracts.

There are upsides and downsides to using lawn care contracts as we will see in this discussion. The more you know about the up and downsides, the better informed choice you will be able to make about if you should be using them in your lawn care business.

A lawn care business owner wrote "I've been in the lawn care business for several years but never have gone real big. For the past 10 years I have been at my new location and my lawn care business is growing. I think I'm at a point where I want to start using lawn care contracts with my customers but I am not sure how to break them in.

I'm thinking month to month lawn care contracts, but I'm not sure if I should do 12 months and figure in leaf removal, spring cleaning, gutters, mulch, etc. I want to continue to offer all services. Any suggestions would be greatly appreciated."

Why not introduce them by having your new customers sign

annual contracts at first. Get the hang of selling the usage of lawn care contracts and then maybe next year, get your other lawn care customers on board too?

"I'm looking for a set monthly income, if their is such a thing. If this works like I'm thinking, the lawn care customer would pay a lower amount per month for more services across a 12 month period. Is this a good idea, yes or no? Easier billing, I think? What's your view on that?"

Another lawn care business owner wrote "Annual lawn care contracts can be very good, but like everything else it will have a downside as well. It seems there is no "standard" way to run your lawn care business in this industry. I've met guys that are perfectly happy to charge per cut, work all summer & take the winter off so to speak. I've met guys (like myself) that have set the majority of their customers up with the same monthly price year round, and I've met guys that set their customers up annually but charge say $100/month in season & $40/month in the off season. (that didn't make sense to me either?).

My 1st year (I started in late, LATE June) I worked by myself. I picked up a lot of per cut lawn care clients. Going into winter I only had 12 annual lawn care customers paying in & about 40 per cut clients. I couldn't make ends meet, So I worked a 2nd job through the winter.

Going into the next season I pushed the contracts real hard with my newer clients & by the end of summer I had 50 annuals & about 55-60 per cut properties. In the winter it made it nice, but the down side was in August & September most lawns were serviced 5 times, I had a 3 man crew by that point. So there was a lot of labor, maintenance, & fuel expenditures for the month & despite the fact that they were some of the best grossing months I'd had to date, money was tight & we were kinda close to not making payroll on one or 2 weeks! It blew me away, I kept looking at the books going what the hell?

When you average out the money it's nice on the back side where the cash flow well outweighs the expenses, but in season it flips on you & goes the other way. You have to be prepared. I found at that point it's the per cut clients that are vital to your businesses cash flow. Now I am carefully keeping a good balance of both per service & annual customers."

What advice do you have for those newer lawn care business owners who are trying to push contracts? How should they go about doing this? Also what % of the customer base do you feel will balk and either not sign or want to cancel you? If they are really against contracts, how should you handle it?

"I think every lawn care client can see the value in essentially financing out the heavy expenses of the growing season over the coarse of the year as it makes it more budgetable for them. There are I'd say 50% that stay on a per lawn care service pay plan, usually for one of a few reasons...

Either they are renting & may not stay there a full year, maybe planning to move? They may not be financially stable enough to commit to anything at all other than "well, cut it now, I'll pay you now & we'll take it from there". Typically if the home is for sale or if they are renters I won't do an annual agreement with them. I might if it is up for sale depending on what time of year it is (there's no way I'm signing on an annual lawn care account that's up for sale in say June. You could work all summer for the lesser rate, & if the house sells in October... your screwed).

There may be a few that will balk at a "contract"... You don't want those people on a contract anyway, they're the ones that will cancel on you. I've only lost 2 annual contracted customers. One was because she didn't want her lawn cut as often as most lawn care customers do & then at the end of the year felt she didn't see enough value for her money…? Go figure. I tried to renegotiate but she wasn't interested & now she is back to being a per cut client.

The other was this month, the man's wife past away & he is moving to be closer to his family. He thanked me for all my hard work & gladly paid the early cancellation fee.

Yes, you need to budget & know what to expect. My issue was most of my lawn care customers came on board during the Spring & Summer this past year. So I wasn't receiving any money from them to budget with during the off season.

It was a little tough. It is like I said in another post, growing pains and a lesson learned. I think having a good mix is best & I'll continue to grow my business as such."

This is another very good point. If a newer lawn care business owner gets his clients on an annual contract and they break it mid season, the lawn care operator can find themselves in a bad spot financially.

"Thanks guys you've both been a big help and have given me some things to think about. I was leaning towards charging per cut only but I think a good point was made in saying that there might be a balance to the both. I think I'll do as Steve had said and keep our per cut lawn care clients the same and any new ones try and push the lawn care contracts. We'll see how it works."

What freebies work to get lawn care contracts signed?

When you are trying to get a new potential lawn care client to sign up with an annual lawn care contract, sometimes you may want to offer some kind of inducement to get them to jump on it. That is exactly what was being discussed in a post at the Gopher Lawn Care Business Forum. Maybe some of these ideas will help you craft your own lawn care contract promotion.

One of the members asked "What are some good specials to offer new clients to sign up for an annual lawn care contract? Like one month free with signed contract? I know different people react to different offers. Let's say I did offer the one month of free lawn care?

For example:

- Jan - cut one week free
- Feb - cut one week free
- Mar - cut one week free
- Apr - cut one week free…..

That would equal a month of free of lawn care service but it would be divided up into those months. Do you think that would work?"

A lawn care business owner responded "I would make it the last month free. It's the only way to be sure you get the other 11 paid in full. If you give it to them quickly and they split after 6 months then you are out!

Another said "yeah I have noticed, when you do a verbal agreement for 12 months and shake hands, you tend to get burned in the winter season. Ultimately the goal of the contract is that you are making money in the winter months.

We lawn care operates have to make a living also. We have bills, we have a family to feed, mortgages and all just like anyone else. I guess some customers don't care or understand. They still have there job in the winter."

A third member added "As far as what to offer for yearly contracts, to be honest, the only way to find out what works is to test different offers. A free month's lawn care service is a great thing to test, but you never know how it might compare to something like a free core aeration and over-seeding in the fall. Or a free gutter cleaning. Or maybe even a restaurant gift certificate.

Again, you never know what will work best until you test a couple of different options."

You might want to consider these options and scale them up as needed. There is no sense in giving more away than necessary.

Customers.

How many welcome letters should each lawn care customer get?

I am constantly learning new things on the Gopher Lawn Care Business Forum. The things that amaze me the most are the things that I just would have never thought of without the help of others. Take for example this simple topic. How many welcome letters should you send to each of your new lawn care customers? I would figure one would suffice. However, when we started talking about it, I learned that other lawn care business owners were sending up to FOUR! Four welcome letters at different times to a new customer! Who would have thunk!

Initially I was talking about a concept where each new lawn care customer would get a letter specific to their needs. However as we got into this the discussion grew and taught me as your lawn care business grows, so does your need to change your marketing. As your client list grows longer, you are probably going to be afforded less time to individually customize your marketing for each client. Instead you will find a need to create more generic material that can be used for all of the new customers.

A lawn care business owner wrote "Our company is a little to big to customize our marketing. With 15 lawn care technicians and an average of 25 lawns per technician, it would be difficult to keep track of.

I think making sure the customer is well informed on how your company handles different situations would help with customer retention. In my welcome kit, I have tried to include answers to every question they may have.

I started my welcome kits in July. Next month I will do an analysis on the retention rate from the customers that received a welcome kit to see if it really has any affect."

Do you mean you include a general list of business frequently asked questions? Like who to contact. How you bill etc. Or do you mean more like lawn specific problem questions?

He responded "Both. It contains the frequently ask questions about how we do business & answers about how much the lawn should be watered, mowed, etc. Also answers about what to do after the applications, and if they come across any problems with their lawns."

Then another forum member joined in and shared "I can see how sending a personalized letter with specifics about the property could be very beneficial, but at the same time it's almost too much work.

I think he hit the nail on the head in the sense you want to create materials that are reusable and duplicative. Instead of taking Before & After shots of that particular customers lawn, using 'any lawn' you've done previously should be enough to convey the story you want to get across.

Also, consider sending a few 'welcome' letters.

   * One immediately after they sign the contract.

* Another before the first service visit, this could be your 'Welcome Kit'.
* Another immediately after the first lawn care service visit.
* And then maybe another one a week later.

Each one would contain something different that cements the relationship, reminds the customer of all the benefits they'll be receiving, and potentially even upsells or lets them know about additional services you offer as well.

Ultimately, it comes down to building a relationship with the customer and viewing them like a person, not a transaction. The instant they become simply a transaction is the instant they're on their way out the door as a customer. Especially in today's economy."

Another owner said "that is a good point. I think I will look into doing that also. Maybe by sending them a survey to see if we have met their expectations so far, or to see if they have any questions we may be able to answer."

How do you suggest coming up with a list of frequently asked questions, to answer?

"I always suggest sitting down and making a list of general questions. Ideally they're ones that come up frequently, but it could also include questions that we might think are extremely basic.

One thing to remember is that it's easy to assume people know the basics about what you do. In most cases however, people don't have the first idea so my rule of thumb is never assume anything."

So the next time you sign up a new lawn care customer, you will be well equipped to do the best you can to retain that customer for the long haul and make them feel appreciated and wanted.

When should your lawn care business send thank you letters?

Reaching out to your lawn care customers and letting them know they are appreciated is very important. This is all too often overlooked because the average lawn care business owner is just simply overwhelmed with the day to day activities of running his business. As a small business owner, you have many great opportunities to reach out to your customers and this leads me to a question asked on the Gopher Lawn Care Business Forum. "When should a lawn care business send thank you letters to customers?"

The thank you letter is an important and often overlooked aspect of making your customers feel appreciated.

Thank you notes or letters can be delivered at anytime. For example:

- After signing a new customer to a maintenance agreement.
- At the end of the season.
- After signing or completing a big job.

- After they have referred someone else to your company.
- Anytime you want to thank your customer or just remind them that you are still here.

Thank you notes should be brief and to the point. Consider a card or postcard to say thanks. The note may be accompanied by a small gift in special circumstances however do not include marketing material. It would seem like you are trying to sell them something under the pretense of doing something nice. The purpose of the thank you note is to do a nice thing for the sake of doing it so leave out the flyers or other advertisements. That being said there is nothing wrong with following up after a couple of weeks with some promotional material.

The above information relates to a specific thank you note however always remember to thank you customers for their business is all your correspondence to them.

So go out and get printed up some lawn care business thank you cards and the next time these opportunities present themselves where you can make the customer feel appreciated, jump on it!

How to come up with your lawn care customer base goals for next year?

If you are like most lawn care business owners, you want to see your business grow over time. How are you going to do this though? Do you have a plan? What are your lawn care customer base goals? That is the amount of base customers you want to be servicing weekly.

I asked this question on the Gopher Lawn Care Business Forum and got a great response I wanted to share with you.

One of our members wrote "To develop a lawn care customer base goal, a lawn care business owner needs to start with time management, this is very important. How many customers can they handle in a normal work week and how eager are they. After they have the first season under their belt then they can analyze how many more customers they can handle. They can decide how fast they want to grow. This depends on the individual business owner. For me, if I was to just do lawn cutting and basic light landscaping I wouldn't want more than 30-40 weekly full time lawn care customers. This would leave me time to do mulch and other services for those customers and still have personal time. This would be ample customer base for a 1 man business. If the one man show started with 15 full time customers, the next season he should set his goal to add at least 5 more full timers."

How many customers should a lawn care operator then shoot for if they want to take on an employee? What kind of range would you suggest?

"One of my friends in the lawn care industry has 135 customers with a mixture of commercial and residential. He has a 2-3 man lawn care crew, so counting him there are normally 4 men. They stay pretty busy yet he recently called me to do some mulch jobs for him because he was swamped.

I wouldn't do more than 35-40 lawns per one man crews. With a 2 man crew I would suggest between 90-100 lawn care customers if they are balanced commercial and residential. If most of the business is commercial or industrial, I would say it would be less because of the time constraints to mow larger properties and perform the other services offered. In the winter months if there isn't any snow plowing going on he keeps his employees busy scraping or doing odd jobs."

I hope this information helps you develop your lawn care customer base goals for next season.

Lawn care customer routes - How far should you drive?

How far out of your way should you drive to service a lawn care customer? Is it smart to take on new customers outside of your immediate service area in hopes of expanding your lawn care business or is it going to hurt your lawn care business and drive up your expenses? Let's take a look into this discussion that came up in the Gopher Lawn Care Business forum.

A lawn care business owner wrote a great question about lawn care customer routes. He asked "what is the farthest you have driven out of your local lawn care route for one customer? I have a lawn care customer that would also like for me to take care of her mother's lawn. Her mother's property is about 20 minutes outside of my lawn care route. The property would take me about 45 minutes to mow. Once I am in that area there is a potential to pick up more lawn care customers in neighboring developments."

Here are some of the responses we got to this question. "If I were to go that far outside of my lawn care route, I would charge a little more because it's only her. Just let her know that she's the only one in that area. If she could get a few people to join up you wouldn't have to charge so much. Also you could distribute some lawn care flyers door to door in those local areas around her."

Another member said "Ehhhh, it depends on how bad you NEED the lawn care business man. Think about it. You could distribute lawn care flyers there & pick up a few more lawn care accounts, but you could do the same in your back yard & pick up a few more close to home. Even if you get 10-15 properties out there, it's always gonna be out of the way. Then what if you get a call from a potential client 5 miles further out than them? Do you go since your almost there anyway?

At some point you should draw a line in the sand & say THIS IS AS FAR AS I GO. A one time landscape job might be different but for a trip you'll be making weekly.... drive time kills lawn care businesses daily."

That was really well put. Survival is survival. If you need the extra work, do it. But I think this point really brings up what your competitive advantage is and part of what it should be is you service a specific service area that allows you to keep your lawn care prices within a competitive range. The further you go out the more you have to charge to cover your costs.

If you focus within your immediate area, you can build up the illusion of your image more. You can appear to be all over town all day long and people will think your lawn care company is bigger than it may be. The more times they see you out and about, the more impressions you will make upon them. At a certain point you will reach that magical number where you could potentially hit the top of mind awareness point and people will call you first when they need lawn care.

"You can charge more for that lawn care customer and hopefully get it! On the other hand, her mother could locate a local lawn care guy that also services the same area as the the original account and possibly lose both. The fact that you were referred hopefully means you made an impression on the client. If the referral is based on your lower price per square foot marketing than only you can figure your cost's and decide.

Scope the referral area and check income levels between point A and B. You might find an over priced market by a competitor that's prime for you to step in and handle."

So remember, think about these topics next time you are tempted to provide lawn care service outside your immediate service area. There are pros and cons to the choice, so decide which works best for you and your lawn care business.

How to improve your lawn care customer retention rates.

Every year a lawn care company is in business they will lose a certain percentage of their older customers. They may lose customers for many many reasons but one thing is for certain, each lawn care company will have a specific customer retention rate. That is the percentage of how many customers they have this year compared to last year. It's important to have a high customer retention rate because it can cost ten times more to generate a new lawn care customer than to maintain an existing customer. As we will see, if you focus on a certain type of customer, you can improve your retention rates.

I asked members of the Gopher Lawn Care Business Forum what their lawn care customer retention rate was and many had very insightful answers. Compare and contrast your lawn care customer retention rate with theirs.

What is your companies retention rate each year?

One member wrote "We have about a 75% - 85% retention rate."

While another shared "For our monthly clients it's about 90% retention, for weekly and bi-weekly it's about 50% retention. I break my customers down into three different categories.

- **Weekly** customers are people who want work done every week but then cut your neck in the winter.
- **Bi-weekly** are every other week in the growing season and then drop you during the winter.
- **Monthly** are clients that pay a set fee all 12 months. When I give a bid I try to steer them to monthly through price. Like $100 a month, $30 a visit, $35 every other week.

If a client wants any thing but monthly they are probably trying to save money. I also don't give them the service that a monthly lawn care customer gets. You know in most cases as soon as the grass stops growing then they don't pay and I don't allow people to call me a month later for service just so they can save a buck. If you wait that long then you need a new contractor."

Another lawn care business owner said "I haven't checked but those numbers seem to be close to what mine would be. I think monthly customers who are willing to sign a lawn care contract, want long term service right from the get go, so it's easy. They are not going to do it themselves, so show up as scheduled & keep them happy and they will stay with you.

Weekly per cut clients often want services on weird schedules so I tend to stick to my guns. Through the growing season I service weekly at price "A" or bi weekly at price "B" (on set scheduled days). I don't play the "we'll call when we want you to come out" game & I'm not calling them every week to see if it's "Ok to come today". So I tend to drop those clients. Some others only want service for short periods of time like say the really hot months….? & that's fine, I've found ways to get even those customers to call me back next year. The weekly people come &

go more often and that's why I (& I think most of us who have been in it for a while) prefer monthly clients. It's an ongoing relationship month in month out, season in & season out. Your their landscaper. I find it easier to maintain a healthy relationship with my annual (monthly) clients."

A Gopher Forum member responded "My view is with a price there comes value. With value there comes a price.

I am the most expensive guy on the block and I have a 95% client retention rate. What I offer my clients is what they pay for and more.

I had a company go to every one of my clients with an ad stating that they would offer a quote 10% lower than their current provider. I had clients calling me telling me that this company was doing this cutthroat approach. So I asked them why they called and why they would not switch? They said that they expect to pay more for the level of service I provide."

Another forum member shared "last year our level of business at the start and as the season progressed had us kind of scrambling to get it all done all season long. I inherited some accounts at the beginning of the season and they were woefully under priced in my opinion. I raised prices considerably across the board, but to help alleviate the sticker shock I offered the fifth mow and tenth mow free. I now, this year, have prices where they needed to be and my customer base is used to paying these prices. Retention rate is at or above 99% as well with our only lost account coming from an elderly woman selling her house and moving away."

As you can see many lawn care business owners find they can improve their lawn care customer retention rates by servicing customers who are willing to sign up for an annual contract and are not looking to price shop. Consider this as a way to screen new potential customers when they call.

Holiday cookie lawn care customer retention idea.

We have been talking about how to start up different kinds of businesses on the Gopher Lawn Care Business Forum and it got me thinking. What if you or your gf/wife always wanted to start a bakery kind of business but wanted to start small at first. Maybe you wanted to start with cookies. You could create a website and then promote it on the cookies somewhere. I bet you could also sell this holiday customer cookie idea to other small businesses in the area if you had extra time and things were slowing down. It could be a great money maker.

What if you started baking holiday cookies that you gave as a gift to your lawn care customers to help build a better bond with them and increase your customer retention rates? You could get a bunch of holiday tins that could hold the cookies. Maybe you could get different sizes. Small tins for smaller customers and larger tins for lawn care customers who pay you a lot more than average. Possibly your commercial account customers could get a larger tin and maybe even a gift card in it for a local restaurant.

Especially with your bigger clients, you really want to keep these people happy.

Inside the tins at the bottom, you could include a holiday card and maybe two 'friends and family' referral coupons for a free lawn cut for new lawn care customers only. This would be a great gift your current customers could give to their friends and neighbors. Another benefit of putting the card at the bottom would be if the customer re-gifted the cookie tin to someone else, you would still be reaching out to a new customer who could use the coupons themselves.

If you are giving a large tin to a commercial client, you might want to individually wrap each cookie and place a sticker at the bottom of each one that could promote 1 free lawn mowing. For use by residents within your town and a yard no bigger than X sq ft. Cannot be combined and valid through a certain date. These could then be placed at the front desk of the facility for the employees or visitors to take.

Maybe you could even give a commercial facility two cookie tins. A smaller one for your contact there and a larger one for the front desk.

Experiment with these ideas and you will find something that works perfectly for your situation.

Lawn care customer retention gift idea.

Recently we have been talking about how new lawn care customers should be sent a letter and some type of gift to help improve customer retention and minimize buyers remorse. Ideally this should be sent within the first month of service. An inexpensive gift idea that you can make is a collection of greeting / thank you cards. These cards could include photos you have taken of local landmarks. On the back of the card you can give yourself photo credit, with your web address, below a description of the photo. This is a nice and subtle way to further help promote your business.

Here is what you do. Find local historic sites in your township or local area. Take a picture of it and create a blank card. It could be used by your customer in many ways.

Then package a half dozen or so cards and envelopes in a larger envelope, with a customer appreciation letter.

The customer letter could say thank you for choosing us to provide you with top notch lawn care service. To show our appreciation, we have enclosed these cards which feature images of local historic landmarks. Use them to reach out to friends and family. It will show them some of the landmarks that make our town unique. These photos were taken by Joe Smith, who is an avid photographer. Thank you again for choosing us.

Sincerely, Joe Smith

You could also give these out to your all your customers at different times of the year. During the holidays you could take photos of holiday decorations around the town.

Collections at the end of the lawn care season.

Are you find it difficult to collect on your overdue lawn care business accounts? Are your lawn care customers holding off on paying? Here are some tips and tricks on how to collect payments.

A lawn care business owner asked "last year was my first year running my lawn care business. I made it through the whole season with only one lawn care client failing to pay. Now that the end of the season is here, I have several (previously prompt paying) customers who have failed to pay their final bill. Is this something out of the ordinary or is it common around the holiday season?"

One member responded "this happens to me all the time. Last season I had a property manager owe me $1,500.00 and it took him until Feb to finally pay. And as of now I still have some past due accounts but it is just normal and I know that after a few mailings or a phone call it will finally trickle in. The holidays, the economy and peoples' ignorance are most likely the causes. Just remember it and either don't work for them next season or just accept the fact they are late payers and you definitely have to keep on them!"

What kinds of things should a lawn care business owner do to get those bills paid that are lagging from last season and how long should they wait before they take further steps?

"Well this is what I do. First send the lawn care customer a copy of your invoice with "Past Due" stamped on it. If you hear nothing after a few weeks then you go to a letter and remember to include you "Past Due" invoice (that "Past Due" really scares people its very powerful so always remember to make that stamp BOLD). If this doesn't work you go to a phone call or stop by the house. Be persistent, that's the key people will get so sick of seeing your face of seeing invoices in the mail that they will pay to get it over with. People are either forgetful or ignorant, sometimes the original gets lost in the mail and they pay by the second notice sometimes they don't have the money and are embarrassed but eventually do get you the money.

Just don't forget it, and next season if you still choose to work with them raise your lawn care rates for the fact that they are a pain and don't honor due dates. I have some people that pay their bills so fast that I didn't even think they got the bill yet. These are the people that you take care of.

Now as for the property manager that owed me $1,500.00, I was just persistent with him and knew that I was getting on his nerves, I also knew that he was always in other states with his other properties and that he needed me for next season. He was too lazy to find someone else and have to show them around. So I knew eventually he would pay me, but if another month would have went by I would have been seen waiting outside of his house! And going to court isn't always the option because a majority of the money owed is under $100.00. Just chalk it up as timing, holidays, economy, and the fact that you can't dangle the "no more services until your account is brought up to date" factor over their heads, you will get your money just not as fast as you wanted it. Just face it, we landscapers are at the bottom of the food chain and people will pay their other bills on time and get to us when they are ready, not when we are ready. Besides we don't have any bills ourselves, right!?"

Can you tell us, how would you suggest going about raising your lawn mowing rates once you get paid? Should you send out a letter to them the next day saying you raised your lawn prices by X%? Or how long should you wait to notify them?

Also, how much of a % should you raise your rates by?

"A lot of the lawn care customers that I have trouble getting paid from are renters and they have tiny yards. A lot of them pay $20 per cut, so after I would finally get paid for that season, the next season's "Welcome Letter" which I haven't written out yet, would just explain that we are raising our rates due to "the cost of doing business" and I would go from $20/cut to $25/cut, that way if you lose them it's one less headache. If they still want to have you take care of the property then you make an extra $5 for putting up with them.

On this small scale it's too complicated to raise by (%) it's just easier to raise like $2.00 or $5.00 per cut. I would usually go through the summer without raising the rates, as most of my late payers show up for the last payment. But you should just raise your rates starting with the new season, but if you had to raise during the season I would say give 30 days notice, like write a letter saying that as of June 1, we will need to now charge whatever. But I usually do contracts and it's easier to just honor it for their length instead of going through the hassle of a new contract. And forget about charging late fees; just be glad that they pay their bill.

Sometimes the renter will not "re-lease" so you will have to deal with another renter but they eventually pay because they are afraid to lose their security deposit. Which reminds me, don't do any work for a renter without talking to the landlord or property manager, renters in my area come and go, a lot are college kids so they just disappear, drop-out, whatever. I think that one of the reasons that a majority of the bad payers are renters because when I am hired by a home owner I also get a lot of business from "Word of Mouth" and when you get one house you usually get a couple of the neighbors.

So as you can guess if "Mrs. Smith" isn't paying her bills and her house gets skipped this round of cuts all the other neighbors will start to talk and "Mrs. Smith" doesn't want to look bad in front of the neighbors. Then you can look on the bright side, if the yard is skipped a couple of times, then the customer finally gets their bills paid then you have to charge them for a big clean-up, but try to get it up front because they will probably try not to pay this bill for sure."

When you say they may lose their security deposit, how do you mean? Is this a security deposit that they pay to the landlord? If so how will they lose it? Would the landlord have to pay you the fee then?

"Well I am not sure how things work everywhere else, but in my area a tenant is supposed to care for the property especially the lawn and snow. Some landlords will pay for it themselves to keep up appearances but most require the tenant to do it. So if at the end of the lease the yard is a jungle, the security deposit is held and used to get the property back in line, and whatever else went wrong, patch holes in walls… So if you previously spoke with the landlord or property manager, and told them the tenant stopped paying bills and you are terminating services until bills are paid then they will either get on the tenant to pay the bill or authorize you to continue services to be paid by the security deposit (this is for some cuts not a whole seasons worth of cuttings but a few to finish out the summer or whatever it may be) but as long as you inform the landlord or whoever they usually take care of everything because it's their investment, they don't want to make the neighbors angry, or have a bad tenant who destroys their property, in a lot of ways you act as their eyes and ears. So you scratch their back and they will scratch yours.

In the end, when the lease is up, you submit the bill to the landlord or property manager and they will pay you out of the escrow account. Most of the time, if a tenant loses the security deposit, it's due to a lot of things not just the lawn, and if it is just the lawn that the tenant owes the landlord will say something like "you must pay all bills or they will be paid by the security" and then you either get a check from the "Landlord Tenant Act" or something like that or you get the check from the tenant."

Great information! I hope you find this useful in helping you get paid from overdue accounts still holding off from last year.

Estimating & bidding.

New to lawn care? How to bid.

A lawn care business owner who is just starting wrote with a great question. He was curious on how to bid and about what kind of insurance he needs. He wrote "I just am starting my own business in landscaping and lawn care and I was just wondering if you had any information on how you bid jobs? What's the best way to do it? Do you try and beat another person's price and their offerings, or do you stay solid in what you believe the price should be for what you provide?

I've watched your GopherHaul videos and you had a lot of good points on this and it really helped me out. Also, another question I had was, when you start your business do you buy insurance for your whole crew or just for yourself and then do the people working for you have their own insurance? How does that work?"

Let's tackle the insurance question first. You will need business insurance that will cover you and your staff. Give a call to a business insurance company and they will tell you more about the coverage they offer.

Now to answer your question on bidding, one of our Gopher Forum members was nice enough to jump in and share his experiences. He wrote "I do have some years of business experience behind me, so here's my 2 cents on bidding jobs. Except for gauging our local market, we pay very little attention to what others charge and we find that most of our clients do the same. In my opinion, trying to undercut your competition will get you broke. Trying to match the "big boys" will do the same.

The first thing we did was to set a minimum of $40.00 for a basic mow, trim, edge and blow (this was $5 higher than the going rate). Only with 2 out of our 30 properties do we charge any less. These two properties are $35.00 and we edge and trim only. Most people will not shop around if your price is reasonable and people who already have a lawn care service will rarely switch to you if only because you're offering a lower price.

Here is my philosophy. When starting out, your price should be:

1) competitive in your local market.

2) fair to the customer.

3) profitable for your company.

Combine these with excellent service and you will get and keep customers. Hope this helps and best of luck."

What % of bids would you suggest a lawn care operator try to land? Where is the sweet spot so they know they are not charging too much or too little?

"Well, for me, the target is 100%. Of course that will never happen but why not set your sites high. Since May, we have landed all except three of the calls we received. I'm not totally sure why we've done so well. Part of the reason may be that other lawn care business owners can't take new customers. If I were to suddenly stop getting new customers after bidding, the first thing I would have to ask myself is whether or not I was bidding too high. We try to bid in the $60 to $70 per hour range. We also usually bid the first service high to cover the extra time spent to get the lawn to our standards. I say don't build your company on price. Build it on providing superior work and customer service."

This is a fascinating topic. My concern is if you get 100% of the jobs you bid on, is it possible you could be charging more and not know it?

"Wow. That's a great question. I'll have to think about that one a little. My son-in-law wants to bid more than the normal "$1 a minute" rule of thumb but I've been reluctant to do that. The way I see it, if we're getting near 100% of our bids, we're either doing something right or we're bidding low. From our research in the area, we are right on or slightly above average with what most other lawn care business owners are charging. We only have 2 properties that we know were slightly under bid. More often than not, we are making more than $60 per hour (actual work time). I really don't know if we want to push for more until we have reached some of our goals and better established our reputation. I can see asking a premium price once we get in a position where it's not so important that we take on new customers."

I agree with you on this. You presented us all a very good lawn care business strategy. The first thing a new lawn care business owner should be doing is to fill up their work schedule and then you can replace customers with better paying customers as you go.

Always follow up after you submit a lawn care estimate.

Once you are contacted by a potential client and meet with them to bid on their property, you aren't done yet. Remember to always follow up. This applies to both commercial and residential lawn care customers.

A lawn care business owner asked "I was just wondering after someone calls you for a lawn care estimate and you go out meet with them, and then submit a bid, do most of them let you know if you didn't get the job or just kinda blow you off."

A Gopher Forum member responded "a few things will probably happen:

> 1. They will say something like 'Geez, that is higher than I thought it would be.' At this point you can either haggle with the price or tell them, 'sorry, that is the price,' and stick to your guns.
> 2. They will say something like 'when can you start.' They agree to the price and want you to do it.
>
> 3. Or they say "I will have to talk it over with my

husband/wife." Nine times out of ten when someone says that, you probably will not get the bid. Now they will either call you back and tell you yes or no, or will not bother calling at all. I recommend that after a few days to give them a call up and ask them if they had any questions in regarding the bid. It helps get the ball rolling again."

Those responses brought up another great question. "Okay how about commercial accounts, when they are excepting bids and say we're not deciding until the middle of March. Should I call them back then or just hope to hear from them and if I didn't get it will they call and tell me. Or just let it go?"

Another member said "If you haven't heard anything after a while, then I would follow up with a phone call and even perhaps a letter. Always follow up. Sometimes they want to see how interested you are and that just might make the deal for you."

Following up with clients is a great way to improve your chances of landing the lawn care bid. Use your call as an opportunity to go over any questions they might have or any sticking points and close the sale.

Why the cheapest lawn care bid doesn't always win.

New lawn care business owners tend to enter the market by bidding their jobs lower than others. This may initially seem to work but as you try to grow, you will see problems with this lawn care marketing attack plan. The first problem is that you may be losing money on the work you are doing or just barely breaking even. The second problem is that you are most likely attracting cheap lawn care customers who only want cheap service. Cheap customers tend to not want any upsells and they are usually your biggest complainers.

As you try to apply this concept to commercial property maintenance there is a tendency to exacerbate the problem. Larger properties will bring larger estimate amounts. However, you may find yourself so fixated on the dollar value of the bid that you fail to calculate your actual costs. You may also find yourself buying larger commercial equipment and then having to hire a staff. This has brought on the ruin of many a lawn care business.

Some commercial property managers know this is a problem and they hate signing up a lawn care maintenance company at the beginning of the year only to have them go out of business half way through the year. They also won't simply choose the lowest bid because they want quality work. Which leads me to this discussion.

A lawn care business owner wrote "I'm new at running a lawn care business so I didn't think it would be this hard to get started. I get lots of calls for estimates but I never get any."

It's good that you are getting lots of calls. Your advertising must be working.

What are your customer's reactions when you give estimates? Is your price too high or do they say they will think about it and just never call you back?

There are many steps in professional and effective lawn care estimating.

Here are two ideas a fellow Gopher Forum member suggested.

1) **Sell quality.** Don't let potential customers pick someone else simply because your bid is a few dollars higher. Let them know that you do quality work and that you are dependable. Take your potential customers for tours of their lawns as you give estimates. Point out areas that you will pay attention too and show them how you can make a dramatic improvement in their yard.

2) **Be ready to work immediately.** You will find when doing estimates if you have your equipment with you and can work immediately the customer will often say "go ahead" right away. Once they see a quality job they will almost always sign on as regular customers.

Knowing and following all the steps will greatly increase your acceptance ratio.

"The one recent job I got called for was a luxury condo complex. The normal price is $80 to $85 dollars a month on each unit. I bid $70 a month.

The condo property maintenance is handled by a condo association and they range from 24 units to 36 units. The way I found out it was $80 to $85 a unit is by asking some guys that have been maintaining the property for years. The condo association told me they received cheaper estimates but then they said (we go for the best service not the best price.) That's what they say and then end up not giving me work."

So remember, start small, scale up step by step. Build profits and gain an understanding of what you need to charge to make a profit. Only make the jump to commercial properties once you have a firm understanding of how to run your business based on servicing residential properties.

Lawn care business sales lesson.

We can always learn more about sales. Without sales we would have no income and without an income we would have no business. So to boost your lawn care business sales let's have a talk with a fellow Gopher Lawn Care Business Forum member. He used to be a car salesman before he moved on and decided to stop making others rich and start making himself rich. I got a chance to ask him to share with us some of his insight into how a lawn care business owner can improve their sales and here is what he had to say.

"Most any business revolves around sales, and in most cases you will sell something at least once in your life. A simple sale can be broken down into steps. There are many different forms of the steps to the sale but here are the ones I use:

1. Meet and Greet

The meet and greet is the first and most important part of a sale. A lawn care customer is going to decide if they are going to buy something from you within the first 15 seconds of meeting you.

During the meet and greet you should shake your prospective customer's hand, look them in the eyes and state your name and why you are on there door step (or where ever). Remember this customer could lead you to more sales so take them as they are your monthly salary, your child's next meal, the new zero turn mower, etc.

2. Fact Find

When you fact find all you are basically doing is finding out the needs of your lawn care customer. Ask your questions and when they answer just sit back and listen. The best way to lose your credibility is to interrupt the customer when they are talking. The best way to build confidence is to listen and give an educated response to what ever they said.

3. Diagnose

I was always told in the car sales industry, what if a doctor gave medicine without finding out what is wrong with the patient? That would be bad right? Yes it would be awful. Giving a proper diagnosis with each customer can boost profit enormously. This step is the most commonly misconstrued part of the sales process.

Medicine without prognosis is MALPRACTICE!

4. Present

This step is where you have to use those superior vocal tools, those sly words, basically you sell. You need to get the customer excited about the product now. With "diagnose" you have selected the product or service with the customer, now concentrate on selling it. If the lawn care customer says that the service is over priced, you need to overcome the objection, DO NOT SWITCH THE SERVICE OR PRODUCT!!! Switching is not forbidden but should be done only if you are about to lose the sale. Most people feel that they picked the product you are trying to sell them so when you try to switch it, they feel that the swindler salesman you are is trying to screw them and rip them off. Do not switch unless necessary.

5. Ask for the sale

Don't be afraid to ask for the sale. This can be intimidating to bluntly say "So ya gonna buy this or what." So you do it with the three yes rule.

You: So do you like the work that I have shown you

Customer: Yes, it looks very nice

You: Do you like me? What I mean is could you stand seeing me every Friday at 11:00am cutting your lawn? (Chuckle when asking this)

Customer: haha yeah you are ok. The last guy who did my yard only spoke to me when he wanted to sell something haha.

You: Is the price acceptable to you? (if not, find out why and overcome the objection. Do not change your price)

Customer: Your price is a bit high but your work is better quality, so yeah the money is right.

Now that you have three yes's, it is time to strike and ask for the sale. Be bold, stern, and serious. No laughing.

You: The work is good, You like me, The money is right? So do we have a deal. Can Joe's Lawn Care, service you with all of your lawn care needs?

Customer: ummm……..Well…..Yes but I need to talk to my wife I will call you tonight and let you know what she said.

This is a good thing, If you did your job and sold him he will sell his wife. Him needing to talk to his wife is better than him calling you later that night and saying my wife came home and said no. If he does not need to talk to his wife, something is wrong or he is single. Sometimes they will simply say no, sometimes they will say yes. but most of the time they will have an excuse why they can not do it now. But they will call.

6. Close

At some point in the sale you will need to close the deal. This is easy because you have built a rapport with the customer and they have already said yes to the deal. Closing is just a reassurance of your quality and their value for their dollar. At the end after all terms are finished and all papers are signed, shake hands with every one (even the kids). Say thank you and assure them that you are here to help them with anything they will need."

So there it is. How to sell from an ex-auto salesman. Don't forget, you worked hard to get this customer and you are going to work hard for this customer. They will appreciate your work and they will thank you. Be sure to ask for a referral. If they like you and they know someone needing your services, they will pass your name along.

Why your lawn care business needs to charge more.

Your lawn care business needs to charge more. I had a discussion with a lawn care business owner who just recently restarted his lawn care business after having previously shut his doors because he was lowballing and not charging his lawn care customers enough.

He wrote "Hey guys you probably remember me. I have been away for a while. I lost my internet connection but now I am back. I am trying to get my lawn company going again after giving up on it last time. I lost too much money lowballing.

This time I am going to do better. I started out fresh and got a bigger and better truck than the old S-10 pickup I used to use. I am also in the process of rigging up side rails to haul debris and currently looking into prices for mowers. I am still rocking back and forth between new or used lawn care equipment. Currently, leaning more towards used. But it feels great to back!"

Can you tell us a little about what you experienced with your previous lawn care business? What did you learn from that experience that you could share with other entrepreneurs just starting out with their own business?

"Well to start with, I was charging way too little for the time I was on spending on the customer lawns and I was killing myself doing it. Yeah that was a big part of it. I was spending more time and money than I was making. I was too worried about making the customer happy that I was not even thinking of my own financial stability.

My lawn care equipment was not too bad but it was a bunch of stuff I dug out of the trash and fixed up and it got the job done. All in all I have come to realize that I need to charge what I need to make, not what I think is fair or reasonable. The way I see it now is that I am a lawn care business and offering a mowing service some people might not like what I charge but if I get a few good clients that would spread the word, I believe that I could be very successful. It was a learning experience and that would be the best advice that I could give is to make the money you need to make a profit with your lawn care business."

Very good insights! Can you say how much you used to charge for an average lawn and what you charge now?

Also, what advice do you have to offer as to coming up with a price you can profit from? How do you create this price now? What factors do you take into consideration that you didn't take into consideration in the past?

"Before I was charging $30 a lawn mowing. But the yards that I was mowing were not really average size. I figured if I could cut the lawn and everyone could see that I was doing a good job, that it would help.

Now when I figure a price it all depends on what is being done. Fuel consumption is big one, time spent on the lawn and the service that is being done. I am constantly trying to review my expenses and what I need to charge. Now I am going to charge in the area of $40 or $45 per average lawn. I will try those numbers and see what happens.

I am thinking about offering additional profitable services like pressure washing. The factors that I am thinking of now that I did not think of before is time. I like to spend too much time caring for a landscape on the property and I tend to do too much. Basically I try to make everything perfect and in the long run I am losing money, not making it."

Thanks for your insight and sharing with us your experience of running your lawn care business. I do feel we can all learn from what you went through.

How to bid gutter cleaning.

If you are looking to submit some bids this season to clean leaves out of your customers gutters make sure you read this first.

A lawn care business owner got on the Gopher Lawn Care Business Forum and asked his gutter cleaning question. He wrote "I have been asked by a neighbor to do a gutter cleanup. She has gutter shields in place but wants to make sure everything is cleaned out and down spouts are good. Her house is 2200sq. and about half of the home has gutters.

I do not think this job will take over 1.5 hours but have no idea what to charge her. I have never done this for money just on my own and folks house. Any help would be appreciated."

Another business owner responded by saying "I charge $1.00 per foot of gutter for a single story and $2.00 per foot on a 2nd story. For people I have lawn contracts with I do it free Spring and Fall. Well free in the sense that it is included in their annual lawn care contract.

I found that a 2 liter soda bottle (cut down) works well for cleaning the gutters. It's pliable enough to get down into the gutter. Take a bucket with you to put the debris in. If you just dump it on the ground, the mess is harder to clean up than the gutters are."

I have been doing a national survey with those who provide gutter cleaning services and the charge of $1 to $2 per linear ft seems to be standard across the country. You would charge more for gutters that are higher up or more difficult to get to than lower ones.

Here are some common beginner pitfalls lawn care business owners find when offering gutter cleaning.

- "On my first job, I just emptied the gutters onto the ground. It took me about 25 minutes to clean the gutters and over an hour to clean the mess from dumping the debris. It was on the walls, the ground, the windows, etc. Since then I have taken a bucket to empty the debris in."
- I used to charge by the hour for gutter cleaning, now I charge around $1 per linear foot.
- If the gutters are easy to reach I charge $1.00 per foot. If the gutters have trees growing out of them, then its $2.00 per foot.
- The first time I ever cleaned gutters, I brought a power washer and blew them all clean....When I went down the ladder, it was a mess, lawn, house windows, screens, everything!!! Let's just say that those people got a free home power-washing!!! Learn from mistakes, right?

Remember to review the job site before you create your estimate. Are the gutters on the first floor or the second? Do they have weeds growing out of them? Are you going to be able to reach them? Use a scoop to clean the gutters and empty the scoop into a bucket. Minimize your cleanup time. Charge between $1 and $2 a ft for gutter cleaning and you should be alright.

How to price Spring and Fall lawn care cleanups.

With Spring just around the corner your lawn care business will be asked to bid on yard cleanups but heed these warnings so as not to go broke while trying to make money.

A lawn care business owner had an interesting experience with bidding her first Spring cleanup and she learned a very difficult financial lesson we can all learn from.

She wrote "Hi guys! I need some advice. I have a very new lawn care company... It's just me and my husband right now. I went out and gave a family a quote for lawn care and leaf removal/lawn clean up. They signed up for annual lawn care service, but needed the leaf removal/lawn clean up asap. So we went out today and I only charged them $70 dollars for the entire job. The yard was moderate size. I only thought it would take an hour....hour and a half tops. HOLY CRAP!! That was wayyyy too low!

I didn't realize until we got out there and into it that the leaves hadn't been raked or picked up in years. We started at 10 am and didn't get done till 1:30pm We had to make another trip back to the house to pick up the 18 bags of leaves and debris. lol I wanted it to look great so we did it right, but it took a while!

So once you got past the top layer there was matted down leaves/dirt/old pine straw. I know hind sight is 20/20 but....What would you guys have charged for that job? How do I go about not under bidding next time?? I know one things for sure...I don't know if I'll be doing any more yard clean ups soon!"

Another business owner suggested "when I get cleanups or junk removal calls I get out my pitch fork and rake and physically turn the pile of leaves over. One of the biggest problems you may find especially where people dump grass trees and clippings is what's under them. In some cases it could be car parts, household trash even offcuts of trees and branches. Once I know this I can estimate the time. The other thing to consider when quoting is how far you need to cart the brush to load it on your vehicle.

I sometimes discount when I can drive my trailer up to the actual pile to load it. If it all needs to be bagged and carried out then add an hour for a big job. You also need to think about disposal fees I have a price per trailer load. This is based on the landfill price /ton min (if they charge by the trailer load you can make on it) the price allows an allowance /mile for gas based on vehicle running costs with a 10 mile round trip minimum. It finally includes an hour for my time unloading. That way I say to people it will be 2-3 hours plus expenses of $X per trailer load and you don't get trapped by having to cart more away than they pay for."

This is a great learning lessons! Great great stuff and you lived to try it again another day so no harm done. You initially thought the yard leaf cleanup would take 1 - 1/2 hrs. But when it was all done it took 2 people 7 hours total! Initially you were going to charge $70 for 2 people for 1 hour of work. So that would be $35 per man hour. Now knowing what you know, it should have been (7hrs * $35) = $245.

"That is absolutely correct! I think at $245 I would have felt much better leaving that job! LOL From here on out I will know better when it comes to bidding leaf and yard clean up jobs. I don't think my hurting back would let me forget! I want to be fair in my pricing for my customers BUT I also want to make sure our pay for the job is fair as well!"

So in conclusion think about your bid time before you give the bid to the lawn care customer. What you may think will take one hour could easily take you seven hours. Remember this example and you will be much farther ahead of the game than someone who doesn't know.

How to price residential snow plowing jobs.

With winter here and a lot of people losing their jobs, many are looking for additional ways to make money and offering snow plowing or snow shoveling services is a great way to get started.

I was contacted by a new lawn care business owner and he asked "I have always wanted to start my own snow removal and lawn care business but I guess you would say I'm green when it comes to it. I kinda have a good idea on what I need on the lawn care side but I would really appreciate any help I could get with the snow removal side any and all help would be great I already have a snowplow on my atv but I know that's not gonna cut it....

Any help with types of equipment and help with salting, sanding, and how to price snow plowing jobs? I would like to jump on this and hopefully get into in sometime this winter. The problem is I live in northwest Indiana and the winter snow storms are scattered and hard to predict."

Another business owner offered this advice. "First off you could find a bigger snow plowing company in your area and sub contract for them doing side walks. Maybe charge $20 - 30 an hour. The beauty about this is no extra snow plowing equipment is needed.

As far as estimating for your snow removal services, here are some ideas on residential snow removal prices.

Charge Labor + Material when it comes to snow

* $110.00 hr Atv with plow
* $40.00 hr Shoveling
* $12.00ea 50 lbs Salt bags
* $20.00ea 50lbs Calcium bags

Example: You get a drive way lets say is 40' X 12' + the sidewalk is about 50 feet long. A job like this will take about 1hr for one man. About 15 mins with the atv to get the drive way done and about 30 mins to do the walk. You will have to shovel the walks because your 50 inch plow will not fit on the walks. And is not safe running a 50 inch blade on residential walks because you can damage the lawn when plowing the walks. Lets say the customer wants salt applied to the walks and drive. I would use about 2 - 50lb bags for a size like this. And this will run about 15 mins. So I would bill this person this way

* 1/4 hr Atv with plow $27.50
* 1/2 hr Shoveling Labor $20.00
* 1/4 hr Salting $10.00
* 2x 50lbs Salt Bags $24.00
* Total: $81.50

That's for 1 hr's worth of work. Snow removal is not cheap and it cost money to fill up your Atv. It costs money to haul your atv, and it costs money to buy bags of salt. And always round your time of labor up. For instance 10 mins will be 15, 42 mins will be 45mins. Try to market your snow service to the higher end neighborhood. Not everyone can afford $81.50 for one hr of your service. Is also a lot cheaper running a snow blower than a atv."

I hope this discussion sheds more light on how to market and charge for residential snow plowing.

How to charge for landscaping maintenance?

It's important to find a niche when you run a business. Some business owners in the green industry focus on cutting lawns, some focus on hardscapes and some on pondscapes. But what if you want to focus on landscape maintenance only? How should you charge for such a service? That is a question put to the members of the Gopher Lawn Care Business Forum. The member wrote "how do you charge for landscape maintenance only?"

Great question and we got a great bunch of responses.

One business owner suggested "well you got the choice of hourly or by the job. If your just starting out I would suggest that you do it hourly for the first few jobs just to get an idea of your time. When you do it by the job your still going to figure in how many hours it will take you. Then you have to add any material into that and give them a price. Most people charge in between the $40 and $60 an hour range."

Another member shared "There is a lot that goes into figuring out what to charge. It depends on your specific overhead costs, what your plans for the future of your business are, and what your local market will bear.

First part of the equation is your overhead costs. Even if you're a small operator just operating out of your home or garage and have no employees, there are still overhead costs involved that you need to account for. Things like vehicle maintenance, equipment maintenance, advertising costs, cellular phone costs, fuel, etc.

Start by figuring out what the average cost for those things are per month. Then assume the average month has about 180 hours of work, if you work 40 hours per week. Divide your total overhead costs per month by 180 and that would be how much you need to make each hour you work - just to cover overhead. But even that is a little inaccurate because even though you may put in 8 hours in a day, you can't bill customers for things like drive time. So your billable hours each day are more like 6 hours. So take the overhead figure and add 20-30%.

That's only part of the equation. That figure above only gives you enough money to just cover current overhead. The next step of the equation are your future plans for the business. Some guys say, "I make plenty of money charging just $35.00 per hour. I am a small operation with little overhead." Fine. That may be true. But what are your long term plans? Do you plan to grow the company? Do you always want to operate out of your garage? Or would like like to have an actual shop one day? Do you always want to use the equipment you have currently? Or would you like to buy some new, better equipment one day? Do you always want to drive that one truck you have now? Or would you like to add another truck and possibly an employee one day? If you plan to grow at all, then you need to charge AS IF you already have those expenses. That is, if you need to make $15 per hour to cover your current overhead expenses, you'll probably want to really figure in another $15 per hour for future expansion money.

The third part of the equation is what your personal expenses are you need to cover each month. Rent, groceries, etc. Let's say you need to make $1,800 to cover your part of the rent (or mortgage), groceries, clothing, etc. So divide that $1,800 by 160 hours and that's how much you add to your hourly rate just to cover your own expenses.

Now you add part 1, 2, and 3 together and that's the hourly rate you will need to make if you plan to work 40 hours each week, be able to afford to grow your business, and be able to afford your current lifestyle.

The final part of the equation is what the local market will bare. People on the rich side of busy metropolitan cities are willing to pay a LOT more for yard work than people in a small country town. So you have to figure out what people in your area are paying or willing to pay. In addition to that, you have to realize that small operators generally can't make as much per hour as established, well-known companies. So you won't be able to bring in as much as the landscaper who has a well established firm in the area. He might be able to get $60 an hour for his work, while you may find it hard to get even $45.

Now that we've established your hourly rate, you should never bid jobs by-the-hour. The way you figure out how much to charge is figure your expenses relating to the job (dumping, fuel, chemicals, etc.) and then figure out how long that job is going to take you. If your hourly rate is $45 and you figure the job will take you 6 hours to do, and the only expense is $20.00 in yard debris disposal costs, then you charge $45×6=270, plus $20 = $290. If you want to play it safe, just in case you are underestimating the time it will take, maybe try $350.00 That's how you bid maintenance jobs - give the customer a total job price.

As for weekly maintenance, that's similar. You don't charge by the hour. You charge either by-the-week or by-the-month. Figure out how long it's going to take and add it all up. If you figure Mrs. Jones lawn is going to take you 30 minutes each week, that's basically 2 hours each month. At your rate of $45 per hour, that's $90.00 per month. Figure in a little for disposal costs and charge her $120.00 per month, or $30 per cut (per week).

That's how most of us do it."

One last thing to add "Make sure you add in some overhead for an owner's "off the tools" salary — in other words, the salary you'd need for managing the business, above and beyond what you'd "pay yourself" for the actual income producing work. For example, I work an average of 10 hours or less a week on the tools, but pay myself average of $500 per week, which is a combo of my "billable" work and my "owner" pay. When you're small, you won't be able to pay yourself too big a salary for "owner pay", but as you grow, add some in, little by little.

It's a way of keeping things "honest" too. In other words, if you aren't making enough to pay yourself well, then something is wrong"

How to charge for snow plowing.

With winter on it's way, many new lawn care business owners are looking to add snow plowing to their list of winter services. Trying to come up with an idea on how to charge can be challenging, especially for new businesses.

A Gopher Lawn Care Business Forum member asked such a question regarding snow plow services. "I have clients asking to have one payment for snow plowing their driveways for the winter season. Is there anywhere that one can get some sort of idea as to the expected snow for the season this year? I have searched everywhere, but found nothing. Realizing that predicting snowfall for any given year is about impossible, I am just wondering if anyone here has come up with an idea to supply this type of service. I did some last year, but lost each of them this year because we only had enough snow to plow 2 times, but they felt they paid a lot for just the 2 snow plows. I realize it is a gamble on both parties' side. I have real estate agents that are requesting a price for a seasons plow so it can be given as an incentive for a buyer, "Buy the house, get a year's snow plowing and mow/trim". Easy to calculate a years mow/trim. Any ideas would be greatly appreciated."

One response was "I charge by the hour sometimes. My minimum for snow plowing small driveways is $35 under 6 inches of snow. Over 6 inches of snow I will charge 40% more. My hourly rate is $125/hr per truck. Salting or sanding the driveway or lot is 40% more. It is hard to price a job when you first get into snow removal. The actual removal is easy. If you have the right equipment you could make good money. I leave an invoice in their mailbox if they are not home, but I knock when I'm done with the job to see if they have cash or a check for me. If not then they have 10 days to send me the money or they will get charge a late fee."

Another response "Here is how we charge for snow plowing: $50 min for residential driveways every 2" of snow fall. So if there is 6" before we can get to them it would be $50 x 3 salt is $2.75 per pound spread.

$X per push on commercial every 2" of snow fall and $3.00 per pound of salt spread.

For ex. we have a commercial customer that has 4 miles of street and 4 mail stations.

We charge them $175 per push every 2" of snow fall this includes 2 passes (1 down & 1 back) clearing cul-de-sac's and clearing mail stations, $3.00 per pound of salt used. Approx 1,000 lbs per application if we do all. We also stated in the contract we are not responsible to clear in front of or behind any cars/trucks street parked. Basically the contract states if the cars/truck get plowed in, we are not responsible to digging them out."

A third business owner added his unique way of charging for snow plow service. "Here's how we charge up in the north east.

The worst winter I've had is 9 storms, the best, 27. We average 12-15 winter storms. So here's the options I offer:

* Per push - each time we come, we charge full time. I do my best to NOT allow any "inch-age" limits (i.e. 2″ then we come out, or push every two inches, etc.) because truthfully, everyone has a different idea of what 2″ is and it's just one more place for conflict. If I have a commercial account and they INSIST on that verbiage, I accept and hope for the best, but I would NOT accept any "cut in pay" if I missed the 2″ mark. We charge full price each push, $15 minimum - most of mine are $20-$25 per push. I charge $5-$10 to cleanup the end of the driveway if needed after the storm.

* (NOTE: I do not offer "per storm". If someone insisted on it, I'd just charge 2-2.5 times my per push rate and hope for the best)

* Per season - with insurance. I don't offer a blanket "per season" charge because there is WAY too much variance in the amount of snow we get. It would be like saying "I'll build you a house for $125,000 and then hoping you decide on a 900 sf ranch and not a 2,000 sf colonial. What I do is figure 15 storms, 2 visits per storm. Let's say it's $25 per push, their contract would be $25 x 2 x 15 or $750. This amount would cover them from a minimum of 11 storms to a maximum of 18 storms. If we had less than 11, they'd get some refund, if more than 18, they'd get a bill. THIS gives them a 90% probability, give or take, of meeting their "budgeted" amount, but also covers us from extremes.

A final word, ALL my plowing is per push, every single one. BUT I think it's nice to have a variety. You get more from the contracts during times of little snow, but you get some big money from the "per push" people during heavy winters. It's sort of like diversifying your stock portfolio."

With those different responses you should be able to come up with a billing procedure that will work best in your area.

How to estimate a bed edging landscaping job.

Are you just starting your lawn care business and wondering what bed edging is and how you should bid such a job? Well we had a great discussion on this topic and I think you can really benefit from it.

A lawn care business owner wrote to us about a bed edging job and he said "I was called by a customer to redo some old mulch beds and make their edges more distinct, bed edging. I started at 8:30 in the morning and laid out where the lawn care customer wanted the new bed edge to be. I then marked the area out with paint and ran a bed edger over the out line. After bed edging you clean all the sod out that has been dug up and is in the beds. Then I used a blower to clean the dirt off the grass after which I added new mulch to the bed.

By 3 pm I had done the edging and some sod clean up and spread 2 yards of mulch. I have to go back and finish tomorrow with 2 more yards of mulch. That's the maximum amount of mulch that will fit in the back of my truck at a time."

What advice do you have for newer lawn care business owners when it comes to creating an estimate for a bed edging job? How should a bed edging job be estimated? By linear ft? How much should they charge?

"On this job I'm doing the edging by the hr and the mulch by the yard. I started with the price for $120 for 2 yards. My hourly rate will change depending on the season and since it's slow now and winter time. I told this lawn care customer I would do the work for $35 an hour.

When I get done I am going to get the square footage of it so I can get a idea how to charge per sq ft for a job. This is the first one that I have done with my new bed edger. I have learned it's way way faster than digging !!!! I will try and develop a price for bed edging per linear ft. One more thing to keep in mind, I used $15 in paint to lay out the lines."

Once you cut the edge and it came time to remove the sod, how did you go about doing that? Did you use a sod cutter?

"If I had a sod cutter I would have but I used a pitch fork by going under the grass and prying up . It worked a little faster than a shovel."

What do you feel is the most important lessons you learned about estimating a bed edging job?

"With this bed edging job I did it by the hour and the mulch by the yard.

Lesson #1 I learned that is a no no. It's to hard to figure out that way.

Next time I'm figuring it up by the linear foot. Also keep a mental note that removing the sod takes the longest time and is the hardest work.

The next bed edging job will go like this.

Layout time. (This Job took 3 cans of paint) and around 2hrs
+
Price per running foot on edging (2hrs)
+
Price per sq foot of sod removal (4hrs)
+
Mulch per yard ($60 per yard)
+
Clean up time (1hr)

I have to work one more day on this job next week. After I'm done with the bed edging job I will take measurements of the linear ft, the sq ft of sod and sq ft of mulch. This will really help me bid better next time."

That is fantastic. It's great to be able to learn from your previous experiences. The first time you do the job you kinda are forced to guess at certain values but afterwards you can then figure out what you need to charge per service to ensure a profit.

Sprinkler head replacement bidding pitfalls.

Replacing sprinkler heads can be very profitable but be wary of potential pitfalls. Know what is involved with the job before you submit your irrigation bid. Let's take a look at this interesting story from our fellow Gopher Lawn Care Business Forum member who told us about one of his irrigation repair disasters.

He wrote "I have under-bid plenty of irrigation jobs in the past. Because I do sprinkler repair, and everything is underground, I've learned that without a "get out" you can find yourself in a no-pay job.

The worst one was 15 years ago. the guy had 10 non-working impact rotors. I normally charge $45 a rotor to replace each rotor, BUT from previous experience with rotor impacts, I assumed that they would be side mounted.

Since I had 10 'easy' rotors to replace I said "$45 a rotor and $20 for each swing joint (I knew due to the design and age of the system that the heads were hard piped)."

So $650 minus $125 for parts = about $400+ (minus overhead) for an hour to an hour and a half job. Good enough.

The guy says OK, I'm on my way to the airport, here is your check. Cool.

WRONG!!!!

Each head had a bag of concrete and rock poured around it (just under the turf) the size of a 55 gallon drum lid. I was breaking rocks like a convict for 10 hours! THEN, I had to load my truck with concrete, with my tailpipe scraping the ground, all the way to the dump!

Moral of the story? If you "flat rate" your pricing per task, include a disclaimer at the bottom stating "Standard Service."

Standard Service means whatever you want it to mean, but for example, if you add a spray head for $85, "standard service means 15 feet, not 300 feet around the retention pond!"

So please keep these thoughts in mind next time you are bidding an irrigation head repair job. What may seem at first to be an easy job, can quickly turn into a disaster where you lose money.

Should you raise or lower your lawn care prices in Winter?

When Winter comes, the lawn care and landscaping industry jobs tend to slow down. Which leads me to this great question that was asked on the Gopher Lawn Care Business Forum. "It's Winter time and work is becoming scarce. So when a customer calls me and I go out to give them a bid I've been sticking to my regular prices for cleanups or whatever it might be.

Does anyone raise prices because it's winter because of less work around?

Lower prices because it's winter to make sure they get the job?

Or just stay the same.

I been staying at my prices but not too many are accepting my bids. I can't really be too picky with jobs now so I try to keep it a little on the conservative side.

When I was busy it didn't really matter if they didn't accept because I had a month long waiting list.

What are your thoughts on this?

Here was one response from the forum "here is my 2 cents worth on it.

    1). I NEVER change pricing from season to season as a general rule.

(Why? because customers talk. If you have customer 1 that you did in November and now a customer 2 in December for the same job like leaf clean up and your rate for the customer 1 was say $45 an hour and now customer 2 is now $65 this may cause conflicts, because customer 1 may have referred customer 2. We don't always remember to ask 'How they heard about us?' but we should make it a habit to ask, and most of the time new customer don't offer to tell us that they were referred by a previous customer.) Does that make sense?

NOTE: I know every job is different. One may have more leaves than another or want some extra work done but when comparing apples to apples, keep the pricing close.

    2). Now this also depends on the status of you and your families well being, if you haven't worked very much and bills are piling up then by all means raise or lower your rates as you see fit. When I first stated my business I went through hard times as do most new business men and women. So this is called "FEAST or FAMINE" and we all go through these times it is the nature of the beast.

    3). The holiday season is here and almost over so things are going to be tight for everyone for a few months. To get more jobs you can offer lower rate for the holidays as a selling point and this will excuse rule #1 and bring you to rule #2. Basically only you know what would be acceptable for doing a certain job, this is all about how much is your time worth? If a job is presented to you and you have a bill to pay and you only charge enough to pay that bill then fine do it, as long as it keeps your head above water.

4). It is hard to do this sometimes but everyone in business especially this industry needs to save for 'Rainy Days'. With the majority of this industry being seasonal 'Feast or Famine' always comes and sits on us for a longer period of time than with other business. My grand-father told me this and I didn't learn what "RAINY DAYS" were until I was like 30 something. I always had jobs and money so I didn't save and found myself in hard times scratching and scraping for work. Just bare with it and hang on tight maybe try some new services to offer to generate some work that may not have been there. Fortunately for me, my wife works seasonal at the IRS and it runs parallel with our lawn care and landscaping season, so we bank her money to live on through the off season months.

I want to also mention, this is good general business advice for everyone. Most of us have gone through this situation or are going through this so the boat is getting full.

One idea we use is a Christmas fund at the bank. Start one and put money in it to cover seasonal living expenses. These accounts draw little to no interest but the money is there in late October for you to move into another account to live from. It works only if you stick to putting the amounts in it each month you set up. If you're short one month and can make it up the next then do it. Don't spend the extra money on something else, you have to be disciplined in this. If you want to continue to be in the lawn care or landscaping business and survive the "Feast or Famine" or "Rainy Days", you need to do this."

Great advice on how do deal with the lawn care or landscaping business when the season slows down. Consider implementing some or all of these suggestions in your business.

Should I raise lawn care prices mid-season?

Many times when a new lawn care business gets started, they tend to under price their services. In order to jump start their lawn care business, they figure if they undercut the average price to mow a lawn, they will quickly fill up their customer base. While this tends to work for an initial jolt, the down side to it is you then find yourself with a lawn care customer base full of low profit or unprofitable lawns. If you find yourself in this situation, how do you deal with it?

One of the member of the Gopher Lawn Care Business Forum wrote "I need some advice guys!

The first few lawn care customers I signed up I in a way... low balled. I read on here that the average rate for mowing was $40 so that's what I charged....BUT the first few customers are military and as a marketing strategy, they get 10% off. Bringing there rate to $35. My husband is in the US Army so I don't mind giving the discount.

Now I have way more lawn care clients (most of them with much smaller yard) and none of them pay that little. I start at $45 and up now. Discount or not. The question is….can I raise their prices in the middle of the season? Or should I just stick it out until next year and then raise those folks. All of them are in an annual agreement with us. Their yards take a bit more time than anticipated and I think they should pay more. I don't want to risk losing them, or make them feel like we are not true to our word and change there agreement in the middle of the season.

What do you guys think?"

One lawn care business owner suggested "I never think it is a good idea to raise prices in the middle of the season. Put yourself in the lawn care customer's shoes. Would you want to be told the price is going up in the middle of the mowing season? I would suck it up for this year and do a great job for those lawn care customers. Then next season raise them a few bucks but don't shock them unless you don't need them. Hopefully they will be pleased enough with your services that a increase won't bother them. Remember there are a lot of lawn care business owners and low ballers out there trying to get your accounts!! I only raise prices in the middle of the season for pain in the butt clients I don't want. The low ballers can have them."

This is a milestone in your business I hope you are aware of that! You are filling out your customer base and you are now looking to get more profit out of them! Congratulations!

I agree I wouldn't raise prices mid mowing season unless they are a problem customer. I'd wait until the end of the season. If you start finding you are getting more profitable customers, you could always potentially drop a not so profitable one if they are too far out of the way. Or send them to another lawn care business in the area. Ultimately you want tight routes with high profits.

We will beat any lawn care quote by at least 20%.

What should you do when you open your mail and see a lawn care business direct mail campaign that says "We will beat any quote you receive by at least 20%!" How do you compete with those willing to drop their prices by at least 20% to get the job. The simple answer is you don't. Let's take a look into how members of the Gopher Lawn Care Business Forum are dealing with such extreme lawn care marketing offers.

One of our members said "I continue to promote my lawn care services, but I am not limited to any one thing and I offer a complete lineup of property maintenance services. I won't waste my time bartering with these customers, there are plenty of guys/gals running around neighborhoods looking for the quick buck that will keep them happy until next week or month.

I also do handyman work and I can schedule these around each other like on rainy days or if I get in a pinch, I have a network of contractors that I trust and can draw on if needed and vice versa. I'm also starting to get emails and calls from asset companies to do rehabs and continued care for foreclosure homes and more and more folks are getting things fixed around there homes these days, so look into what one can offer for services.

In watching other small businesses grow I've noticed the ones that seem to continue to grow always had a couple of irons in the fire, usually related in some way. My old boss owns a logging outfit, then started buying woodlots and now develops them to the point of house lots, then sells them through his own realty company.

I know another guy that offers pressure washing to go with his lawn & landscaping business and that keeps him going.

If one door closes another one opens and I see it all the time. If I'm not offering lawn mowing I will be doing something, whether building picnic tables, decks, painting, doing a remodel, there always seems to be something that comes along just when I need it."

Another lawn care business owner said "my suggestion to all of you is to stand out in front of your client's homes with a pen and paper. Try to write down all the services you can offer to your client, ie; not only the standards like, lawn mowing, edging, line trimming, blow, mulching and flowering but how about small home repairs? Change out the outside lights, gutter cleaning, touch up on home (paint), putting up Christmas lights or decorations, cleaning out and organizing garages and shelving in the house or garage, the list can go on and on. Just use your imagination and stay with in your realm

I just took over a lawn account and reviewed with this client what services I do and gave her a hard copy of it as well so she can reference it later, just in case she needs something done. As we were speaking, she stated that she needs her 2nd story windows cleaned. About 12 of them. I told her that I could do it and it would take me about 2 – 3 hours to do. She said okay and just bill me. I asked her if she wanted to know the price and she says, "No, because I'm not going up there to clean them, (we are outside and she is looking up at them) whatever you charge is okay with me." So tomorrow I am cleaning some windows and adding maybe a service that can happen several times a year.

The number 1 thing you can do that will lead to more you can offer is ask! Ask what other services you need? What are you looking for? How can I help you? You can try to guess, you can try to second guess, but what does that get you? Ask them to think about it and get back to you!

By asking Real Estate companies what they needed, I found that they wanted foreclosed homes cleaned, rugs shampooed, walls with picture hole filled in and re-painted, etc. I also found they need properties winterized. They pay me $50.00 per property ($100.00 if property has a sprinkler system). This is a good extra Fall income!

Their suggestions (wants - needs) can and will lead to new services to offer. So always remember to ask."

I hope these suggestions lead you to talking with your customers more and asking them more questions.

Equipment.

Choosing the right snow plow for your lawn care business.

If you are looking to offer additional services that can help get you through the winter months why not consider offering snow plowing?

When you are looking for a snow plow there are many different options to consider. Here is some advice from the members at the Gopher Lawn Care Business Forum.

One member suggested "I run a 8.5' plow and it weighs in about 880 lbs with mount. You should always go with a wider plow.

1. The minimum plow width should be wider than your tires so you can get traction and you don't pack the snow which allows for easier removal.
2. The wider the snow plow the more snow removed, less time at property = more money.
3. Before the snow hits, you need to do a layout of the property so you know where the obstacles are, and how you will attack the drive. You need to know where the snow will be piled and most important of all, will the snow plow fit.

Snow plow manufactures will only offer one maybe 2 sizes bigger than the vehicle it was designed for. Take mine for instance, a 2001 Chevy 3500 hd 1 ton dually, the company that makes my plow offered a 7.5 ft width (smaller than my rear duals, 8, 8.5 and 9ft. I chose the 8.5ft width because of some driveways I am doing, but if I add wings I gain a additional 24″ making the plow 10′4″ so i can plow the K-mart parking lot quicker."

If you have a smaller truck, you won't be able to mount such a large snow plow on the front of it. So snow plow manufacturers have come up with smaller light weight snow plows. Some of these lighter snow plows come with the ability to apply downward force. You may be wondering what the benefit of this is. I asked what are the benefits of downward pressure for plows on smaller vehicles?

"You have the ability to back drag the drive way. With the lighter plow (350 lbs) you need the downward pressure to help. This is very beneficial when you want to drag snow away from the end of a driveway that meets up with a garage door."

You don't need a truck to start a lawn care business.

If you have been waiting to start your lawn care business because you are saving for a truck, you need to reconsider. There are many lawn care businesses started with just a car. Look at what one of our Gopher Forum members' has been able to do.

A new lawn care business owner wrote and said "I have done little nickel and dime yard work on and off for a very long time and recently decided it was time to make some real money doing it and become less dependent on my current employer that looks like it may fold under the economic stress.

I look forward to learning a lot here. At this point since I do have a day job I am looking to take on some side work mowing yards in my area. Last time I did this I got way too busy and back then my current employer was doing very good so I pretty much stopped the yard work adventure. This time I hope to start of with the mow, blow and go theory for now at least and be much more careful as to not over book myself like I did before. Thus far as much as I can tell I am ready to go. Got my trusty old car and converted boat trailer, mower, weed whacker and blower. Got the business cards, put up fliers and my ad comes out in the paper tomorrow."

That is a fantastic story, can you tell us a little about your equipment setup and how you put it all together?

"A landscaping truck is very over rated. I use as I have always used a 1981 Toyota station wagon to tow my trailer. The little 1.8L hemi and 5 speed has no problems what so ever towing the trailer which is a converted boat trailer. As you can see it's not much but it's cheap and reliable which is all that matters. I can't haul a lot but why do I need more than what I have?

My lawn care business start up costs.

- Car= $150
- New transmission= $300
- Boat $400
- Sold boat kept trailer made a $200 profit
- Materials to box in trailer $60
- Mower $120
- Line trimmer $80
- Blower $69.99

All total I am able to go into business for $979.99. Now take into consideration I already had the equipment for maintaining my own yard then it only really cost me a few hundred total. This of course dose not include business cards, paper to print fliers, computer to hook printer to so on and so forth but as you can see its very easy to get started cheap so common people call me LOL.

I live just outside of a golf course community so I figured that would keep me pretty busy, unless of course yard maintenance is part of their home owners association benefits, I have seen that before."

That is great! What have you been doing to attract lawn care customers?

"To attract customers right now I am running an advertisement in the paper and it comes out tomorrow. The headline of the newspaper ad says something to the effect of *"Pain in the grass?"* mowing and weed eating, call me. It's straight to the point and I think the bold title of Pain In The Grass will catch peoples' attention. I am also putting up fliers and handing out business cards to friends and family. I was also thinking of hopping on my mountain bike and running around my small town and leaving business cards at the doors of houses that looked like they needed the yard work done but I don't know. I keep my yard very nice, I enjoy doing this kind of work but I think I may be offended if my yard was bad and someone left a yard work card at my door."

I hope this story inspires you to start your lawn care business. If you have been sitting on the fence waiting to save more money in order to buy a truck to get your lawn care business started, now you can see how one lawn care business owner has done it without the need of a landscaping truck and you can too!

Low cost enclosed lawn care trailer rack ideas.

How do you secure your lawn care equipment in your trailer when you are out and about driving around town and servicing your customers? Here are a great bunch of ideas on how to construct a top notch and cheap trailer rack system.

One of our forum members wrote "what I am looking for is a rack to hold mixing oil, WD40 etc.

I am about to order a trimmer rack as the final thing I need, I would prefer one that locks easily. I am curious about tools. Do you guys carry a tool box with each setup in the event that something breaks?"

Another lawn care business owner said "I carry a tool box on my trailer all the time. The rack units I use for the inside of my enclosed trailer are from a big box home improvement store and they are cheap. My chain saws sit in a water hose rack with a small L bracket with the end bent up after it was in place. I use a bicycle rack rook to hold up my back pack sprayers.

You should check out the closet organizer section of your hardware store. They have different parts to create a great organizer. You buy the 2 up brackets then you can get as many shelves as you need. I think the price for what I have with the oil and every thing on it ran me around $25 and the rack that's one piece was around $12 and my back pack blower hook is only $2.

It is cheap, great looking and functional, just what we all need.

Don't forget when you are at a job site and you take the equipment out that you are going to use, make sure you lock your trailer back up. I was doing a deck a few years ago in a very good area of the city, we stopped for lunch and went around to the front of the home to eat, 1/2 hour later we went to go back to work around back and most of our tools were gone, I was shocked as we didn't hear or see a thing and were only, maybe 50 feet away so someone was watching."

What great ideas! The next time you are trying to figure out how to organize and manage all your equipment and parts for your enclosed landscape trailer, consider these cheap and effective options.

Things to check before you buy that used mower.

Buying used outdoor power equipment can be a great way to save money but it can also open a can of worms and end up costing you if repairs are needed. How do you know if a used lawn mower is going to be a good deal? That's what one of our forum member's asked when he wrote "I have found a deal on a 2007 60 inch commercial mower with 25 a HP engine. It has 240 hours on it. I have been offered this for $3,000.00. It appears to be in great shape.

This is my first zero turn and I have been looking at many different manufacturers. What should I look for before I decide? I think this is a good deal. Any comments or suggestions appreciated."

Thankfully another one of our forum members is a outdoor power equipment dealer and he knows his stuff. This is what he shared with us. It will help all of us when we are looking at used outdoor power equipment. He responded "first, are you buying this from a dealer or from an individual? If from a dealer, will they give you any warranty? Since you have been looking at new mowers of the same brand, how much would a similar one cost you new? Assuming it has no warranty and passes the test as follows below, I would pay no more than about 60-70% of new price similar piece of equipment. Do you know if $3,000 is the lowest price you can get on it? Have you tried to get a lower price?

Here are some questions I am sure you already know the answers to, but for everyone's benefit I will post the questions anyway.

1. If you are buying from an individual, why are they selling it?

2. Was it used to mow their own yard only? Or was it used for commercial use (to mow more than their own lawn).

3. Can you verify their answer to #2 without asking them directly or even indicating you are questioning their answer ("no longer need this big of a mower", or "decided to get out of the lawn care business", or..... Just think, "does their answer make sense?")?

4. Do they have maintenance records? Will they provide these records to you to preview before the purchase? Will they provide these records to you with the purchase?

5. Can they tell you who serviced the equipment when it was serviced? Can you verify this?

6. If buying from a dealer, have they serviced the mower including sharpen the blades, check the belts, change spark plugs, air filter, fuel filter, and oil?

7. Have they ever serviced this mower before buying it?

8. Did they sell the mower new?

9. Why did the original owners sell it? (Again, think about their

answer to see if it makes sense or not. Typically power equipment dealers are considerably more honest than car dealers but there are a few here and there that may still lie to you....)

10. Do they know if the owners were the caring type?

11. How does this mower compare in price to other mowers the dealer is selling?

12. Will the dealer show you or tell you what the blue book value is for the mower?

13. Does the mower have an hour meter on it so you know it only has 240 hours on it or is this a "guestimation"? (This applies to both dealers and individuals)

Either way, look for these signs of wear, abuse or lack of maintenance:

A. What is the over all appearance of the mower (look for chipped paint, bent parts, etc.)?

B. Do the tires have any signs of being "plugged"?

C. Do the tires appear to have lots of wear?

D. Remove the dipstick to see what the oil looks like (look for black oil, is there enough oil, etc)? If you don't know what black oil looks like, pull the oil dipstick out of your car when it reaches 3000 miles after an oil change. Or, take a mechanic friend with you to look at the mower. Black oil is a sign it hasn't been changed. You want it to look more like maple syrup.

E. Check for loose parts (loose or missing bolts). This is a good indication this mower has been taken apart in the past or that the owner has been abusive with the mower/engine.

F. **Caution, it is recommended that you wear gloves while doing this part of the check up. Also remove the ignition key to prevent anyone from trying to start it while you are doing this.** Reach under the mower deck and grab a blade. Now try to move it up and down, checking for deck bearing wear. Also check for blade sharpness, dings to the blade's cutting edge, bent blades, and large deposits of grass underneath the deck.

In typical cases the oil should be changed once per year or every 100-150 hours, depending on the particular motor. Knowing after how many hours the oil needs to be changed helps you know how often the needs to have been changed. It is recommended to change the oil at least once per year."

Online lawn mower sales scams. Be aware!

Have you ever looked on any of those free internet classified ad sites and searched for some used outdoor power equipment? There are plenty of items to choose from. Just make sure when you do choose one, you can inspect the item before you buy it. One of our Gopher Lawn Care Business Forum members almost got caught up in a scam that he was kind enough to share the details with us. Don't let this happen to you!

He wrote us "I just wanted to update you all on the mower I was considering buying online. It turns out the guy I was dealing with was trying to pull a scam. This mower was found on an internet classified ad site in San Antonio.

He had sent me pictures, model numbers and a storage company that was suppose to be storing the mower for him. He said he had to move to the UK and had left the mower with a secured moving company in Amarillo Texas which is over 600 miles from Houston.

He advertised the mower being in San Antonio. He said this company would deliver the mower to me and give me 7 days to have it checked out before they would release the funds to him. He even was willing to pay shipping free and free pick up if I decided not to buy the mower. All I had to do was send a Money Gram to a guy at this company in the UK. Yeah Right!!!

None of this was mentioned when I first contacted him and before I posted this message.

I am a retired police officer and this brought up a lot of red flags so I asked for the serial number. Told him the bank needed it for the loan. He stalled by sending me the model number but later sent me a serial number.

I called the mower manufacturer and they told me it was a 2001 model and not a 2007 model. They also provided me with the previous owner, a lawn care company out of Wisconsin. I called them and they told me they had traded in a bunch mowers last year and all had over 1500 hours on them. None were 2007 models.

I contacted the seller with the information I had obtained and guess what? He quit responding to my email. Email has even been turned off.

So buyer beware when dealing with used mowers. Never buy site unseen and make sure you are dealing with the owner in person. Call the manufacturer and check on the equipment. they will help you determine the original buyer and any service on the mower they have on file.

I ended up buying a new mower instead."

This is great information and I really appreciate you giving us all a heads up about these online scams.

Powerful website tips.

Where should your phone number appear on your lawn care website?

You would think by the title of this, the story below would be so simple you shouldn't even have to read it but that is certainly not the case. Most lawn care business owners don't put much time into where their phone number should appear. Just ask yourself where on your website does your phone number appear? One of our forum members had some great information to share with us on this topic.

He wrote "You want your phone number PROMINENTLY displayed on your website. You want to make sure you edit your html meta tag description to include your phone number first so your search engine listing will display your lawn care business like this.

ex. how your site would appear on a search engine.

http://www.your-lawn-care-business.com - 111-222-3333 Joe's lawn care blah blah blah blah blah lawn care in Your City blah blah blah blah blah ...."

I asked him what is the importance of having your phone number in that location? Why is it so important?

He responded by saying "Let's say you run a lawn care services in Somewhere, Arkansas.

You would want to make your web TITLE to read "Somewhere Arkansas Lawn Care Service"

Your DESCRIPTION would be (assuming this is your website name):

"http://www.SomewhereLawnCare.com 111-222-3333 Somewhere Arkansas lawn care? We are the lawn service leaders in Somewhere, Arkansas. We specialize in landscaping, lawn care, landscape lighting and sprinkler systems in the Somewhere Arkansas area."

The phone number should show up in the link description on the search engine (depending on the link.)

The customer then won't even need to take the added step to visit your site first, because they found what they want, a phone number.

The easier you make it to have people contact you, the more contacts you will get."

This is great information and I do hope this gets you thinking on how to alter your lawn care business website to display your phone number and contact information.

How to use a squeeze page on your lawn care website.

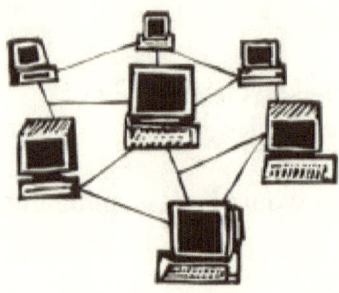

In this discussion we learn how creating a 'squeeze page' on your website can help you collect customer contact information. We also learn what your advertising should say in order to get as many people as possible to want to click through your internet banner advertisement and give you their information to market to them in the future.

A Gopher Forum member wrote "I made a trade with a local advertising business a few weeks ago for a magazine ad in return for me to do her yard for so a certain period of time.

I have been working on her yard off and on since the ad was published.

As much as I advertise on internet social networks, a lot in different ways, another business offered a trade with me, they said I will get a lot of publicity. They want to put a banner with my business name on their website and have it linked to my website. They also want me to write an article in the (ask the expert section) of their website on the topic of fall/winter upkeep advice to help people. I will also be in the coupon section."

One member responded "In terms of the banner ad you are discussing, if you want people to respond you need to give them a reason. Sure, some people will respond because they need something right now, but what about all the people just THINKING about a particular service you might offer? What about the people that already have a service provider, but aren't very happy with them and are considering getting someone else?

If you include some type of offer that gets people to at least click on the banner and take them to your website to continue or begin the relationship building process, you will be ahead of the game. Keep in mind that 'FREE Estimates' or some type of discount aren't very effective anymore because EVERYONE'S doing them."

"Do you have any ideas on what I could put in the banner ad to get a potential lawn care customer to click on it? The ad rotates with others so it only pauses on mine for 2-3 seconds. I currently have on the ad "call for details", but I doubt that would get them to call. Any thing catchy you could suggest?"

He responded "Free mowing might attract a few people, but one thing to remember is that you want to get as many people as possible into your sales funnel. Saying 'Free Mowing' will definitely get a few people to respond, but I bet you'd get even more if you offered a free report titled, '5 Secrets to a Thick, Green, Weed-Free Lawn', then include your call to action like, 'Click Here'.

Then what I'd do is instead of sending them to your regular website I'd set up a special web page called a squeeze page. All it is, is a web page who's only purpose is to get people to submit their name and email address in exchange for this free report. You don't mention anything about the 15 different services you offer or how you've been in business since 19XX, or how.....well, you get the idea.

Then once they submit their information you could take them to your regular website because you now have their contact information and you can communicate with them via email for free.

Remember, marketing is a step-by-step process and if you try to take your prospects from A to Z in one giant leap, you'll lose more than you'll manage to keep!"

Can you give us a little more insight as what this squeeze page is?

"You want to offer the free report BEFORE taking them to your regular web page. It's called a squeeze page and it's only purpose is to capture visitors name and email.

On most websites there are WAYYYYY too many places someone could get lost. A confused mind doesn't act/buy so the key is to create a web page who's ONLY OPTION is to submit their contact information.

Once they've done this, then you take them to your regular site where they can learn about everything you have to offer.

And yes, you want every visitor to fill out this information. However, if you're worried about losing people to this (the number you'll lose will be much smaller than you'd think), simply place a link that says 'Click Here To Learn About ABC Lawn Care' and then takes them to your regular site."

How your landscaping business can make $200,000 in a month.

$200,000 in one month? Is your lawn care or landscaping business able to do that? Well if you're not there yet, read this and find out how to do it.

If you are looking to grow your lawn care and landscaping business you need to think big. Let's take a look into how one of our Gopher Lawn Care Business forum members made close to $200,000 in one month.

We were talking about the importance of internet marketing. Both ranking high in search engine results as well as spending money on advertising.

One of the first types of internet advertising we discussed is something called geo-targeted ads. These are ads that appear on the screens of users who live within certain geographic areas. How does the ad know which computer to appear on? It determines it by using the i.p. address of the computer. This lawn care business owner gave us some insight as to how to create such an ad and their effectiveness.

"You simply create an ad (takes a few minutes), set your bid price, activate geo-targeting inside your Google Adwords account settings, and then you can even go in and tell Google exactly which websites you for-sure want them to go after.

I spend way less than $70 a month to have our ads pop up on website via Google Geo targeting ads.

But I'll warn you, geo-targeting ads don't produce a lot of calls. What really produces a lot of calls is being on top of Google in the organic listings. If you type in landscaping in my area into Google and see who's site comes up on top in the regular (organic) results. That's what produces calls.

I don't have geo-targeting set on all my ads. I don't like those kind of ads much anyway. So I give them such a small bid that I don't care so much if they occasionally appear outside the area I am targeting. I could spend the time to make every ad I have specifically geo-targeted, if I wanted. But the thing is sometimes my clients are away in California or have two homes or are just moving into our area. So most of my stuff is geared more toward specific key words more than it is geo targeted. And I pay so little for those little ads anyway, I don't really care.

My PPC (price per click) main ads in Google and Yahoo, those I pay some serious dough for. The bid price on those is pretty high. But the bid price for these little text ads is like 40 cents and they rarely get clicked on. I spend less than $20 a month on those. So I've never felt the need to really get them totally dialed in like I would like them. It's just additional advertising.

My main advertising is getting my site to the top of the Google organic listings. My fall-back is PPC advertising with Google and

Yahoo. And then I have several other fall-backs to catch people too."

How much do you spend on pay per click ads and what kind of results can come from the pay per click ads? How big of a deal is click fraud when using these kinds of ads?

"It's a little expensive but well worth the results. For instance, last June our Google Adwords bill was a little over $1,350.00. But our total sales just for that month were $186,000. A good half of those jobs or so came from people finding us via a regular Google search. And back then, I didn't know about SEO so my site wasn't coming up on organic listings. It was only coming up via my PPC ad.

As for the click fraud you're referring to. That doesn't happen much, if at all. My analytics program allows me to track every single hit I get on my website, where it came from, what search term they used to find me (if they used a search engine), what their IP address is, which pages they checked out, how long they stayed on each page, what country they are from, what browser they are using, etc. I review that stuff fairly regularly. I've never seen someone who came to my site for just a few seconds (e.g. just to cause me a click rate charge) and left and did that repeatedly in the same day. I might be overlooking a few here and there. But I can tell by reviewing my analytics that most of the people visiting our site are legitimate interested parties and they are spending usually several minutes on the site."

I hope this discussion gives you ideas and goals to shoot for. If you don't have a website for your lawn care business, get one! Remember I have many free lawn care business website templates you can download and use. Also, learn a little about search engine optimization and last but not least, experiment with using yahoo and google adwords for your internet advertising. You never know when experimenting with these different advertising methods will give you a jump on your competitors and make you stand out.

I hope all these stories and insights have helped broaden and expand your business mind. Take all you have read here and go out and apply it. When you learn something new or interesting, please get on the Gopher Forum and share it with all of us. We'd love to hear what you have to say.

Until the next time, always remember to Dream it, Build it, Gopher it!

www.ingramcontent.com/pod-product-compliance
Lightning Source LLC
Chambersburg PA
CBHW031822170526
45157CB00001B/152